. . .

He's a worker. He's a worrier. He's there

to pick you up, five minutes before you really need him.

He's the president—of whatever. He's on the board

of directors—pick a board, any board. He's the owner,

the GM, the producer, the director, the head of the studio,

the priest, the lead guitarist, the pope.

He's also the most remote, inaccessible, bottled-up,

in-denial, opaque, cold-blooded, mercenary,

dysfunctional guy in town.

Meet

THE WHITE GUY

. . .

STEPHEN
HUNT

the
WHITE
GUY

[A FIELD GUIDE]

Douglas & McIntyre
Vancouver/Toronto

Douglas & McIntyre Ltd.
2323 Quebec Street, Suite 201
Vancouver, British Columbia
Canada V5T 4S7
www.douglas-mcintyre.com

Library and Archives Canada Cataloguing in Publication
Hunt, Stephen, 1961–
The white guy : a field guide / Stephen Hunt.

ISBN 978-1-55365-302-8

1. Men, White—Humor. 2. Canadian wit and humor (English). 1.Title.
PS8615.U683W48 2008   C818'.602   C2008-901487-1

Editing by Scott Steedman
Cover and text design by Peter Cocking
Cover and interior illustrations by Kevin Mutch
Printed and bound in Canada by Freisens
Printed on acid-free paper that is forest friendly (100% post-consumer
recycled paper) and has been processed chlorine free.

We gratefully acknowledge the financial support of the Canada
Council for the Arts, the British Columbia Arts Council, the Province
of British Columbia through the Book Publishing Tax Credit,
and the Government of Canada through the Book Publishing Industry
Development Program (BPIDP) for our publishing activities.

For Melanee and Gus,

who both share their deep thoughts with me.

. . .

CONTENTS

. . .

PROLOGUE

· · ·

MY NAME IS STEVE, and I am, *je suis*, a white guy. There. I said it.

I've always been a white guy. I grew up in Winnipeg, a city best known for being cold, flat, boring and home to Canada's oldest ballet company. Maybe not the whitest city on Earth—that would be Brandon, Manitoba—but pretty close.[1] When it comes to white guys—our eating habits, cultural values and general history—I pretty much have it down cold.

By now you're probably thinking, what's the big deal? *You're a white guy. Hello! Is there a problem? God, I'm so sick of white guys whining about their imaginary problems, I'd like to slip a few pitchers of Third World drinking water into the green room before one of those Republican debates. Then white guys would have real problems.*

---

1. There are arguments to be made for Reykjavik, Iceland, being whiter than Brandon.

You'd be right.

After all, if you're white, and a guy, there's really nothing you can't do.[2] Right? Just the other day, my African-American wife Melanee is watching *Entertainment Tonight* and yells out, "Rosie O'Donnell has to be a white man, because no matter what she does, somebody, somewhere still wants to offer her a *job!*"

Does that make any sense to you? If it does, congratulations. You've just taken the first tentative step down the long, winding road that leads to what life looks like if you're *not* white, a guy or Paul McCartney (more on him, John, Yoko and that one-legged ex-model who just nicked him for 25 million pounds, later).

There's a word for this: empathy.

We white guys don't always demonstrate much of that stuff.

Quick story: I recently read a memoir about a Vietnam vet who returned to 'Nam forty years after he left. One day, he finds himself on one of those trails through the jungle that soldiers took, when he comes across another former soldier, a North Vietnamese guy—his former archrival. They start talking, and the North Vietnamese guy starts explaining the whole daily ritual they followed during the war. In places like this, he says, pointing to an overgrown part of the jungle, we would sit at night and our commanders would read American literature to us. Faulkner. Hemingway. Mark Twain.

The American guy, who spent his nights during the war terrified of what he couldn't see out there, asks, *why?*

The North Vietnamese guy says, we were taught that to conquer your enemy, you must understand how they think, so we would read American literature. Then he pauses a moment and asks, "What North Vietnamese literature did you read?"

Who has time for North Vietnamese literature when you can just *bomb* their asses into oblivion?

---

2. I wouldn't recommend a midnight stroll through downtown Baghdad.

COME TO THINK of it, I don't think I even *noticed* I was a white guy until I met Mel.

It all started at a play, in downtown New York City, in 1995. The play, as it turned out, was called *Funky, Crazy Boogaloo Boy*. It was by Ned Eisenberg, an actor who has appeared in such films as *Million Dollar Baby*, and it was about growing up white in the '60s and falling in love with a black girl at a time when you didn't do that sort of thing.

Mel, it turned out, had auditioned for the lead role, and I couldn't work out why they'd given it to some model instead. Mel was my Perfect 10, my Holly Golightly, a unique blend of Lisa Bonet, Anne of Green Gables and Malcolm X.

She grew up in Baltimore, in a world pretty much the polar opposite of mine. She was an integration baby, one of that generation of African-Americans born in the '60s and '70s who grew up, as they say, changing minds and opening doors. For Mel, one of those doors was an open call for a Washington, D.C., production of the Broadway musical *Annie*.

Her mom drove her down the turnpike to D.C. from Baltimore in their old, blue Plymouth Fury II.[3] She was twelve. She was cute, adorable, precocious and verbally gifted. She practically had a neon sign flashing "Child Star" over her head wherever she went.

Alas, she was not enthusiastic about playing Little Orphan Annie.

She sat in the back seat of the car, dressed in a frock dress and an abundant, curly orange wig that made her look like the lovechild of Ronald McDonald.

"But Ma," she says. "There are no black Annies."

"That can always change," Ma says.

"I don't wanna change minds," Mel says. "I don't wanna open doors."

---

3. Dramatic re-enactment of a dinner party story. Make and model have been changed because women never remember the make and model.

When you stop and think about it, who does? It's too tiring. Maybe you pick up some immortality or a Nobel Prize on the back end of the deal, but all in all, most of us would just rather curl up on the couch and watch the world unravel on the evening news.

Two and a half years after Mel and I met, on the same day Rudy Giuliani gets elected to serve a second term as the mayor of New York City, we get married at City Hall in Norwalk, California, under a fake wreath set up in a conference room.

Thanks to Mel, I have a wonderful, smart, breakdancing, five-year-old, African-American, Creole, French, Ukrainian, British, Manitoban, Canadian son named Gus.[4] I have also spent a decade with around-the-clock access to a non-white, non-guy who is prone to saying whatever pops into her mind, and believe me her thoughts occasionally differ quite a lot from mine. That's a mild way of saying we often experience two completely different versions of reality, often at the exact same moment, side by side on the couch watching the very same *Friends* rerun.[5]

LIKE I SAID, I grew up in Winnipeg, being white, a guy and not feeling too bad about it.[6] But by the time I got to college, I had no trouble totally embracing the dominant worldview of the place, i.e., the idea that white guys were the problem with *everything*. In fact, I was so busy studying political science, writing ironic poetry, and befriending social, political and cultural outcasts, I didn't stop to notice how enthusiastically I was embracing an idea that identified *me* as the problem with everything. Know why? By embracing it, I ensured myself one thing that every young man desperately wants to be: not my dad.

In retrospect, that may have been a bit of a flimsy basis for a worldview, but I'm not the first guy to do it. Won't be the last,

---

4. August Ellington Sage is on the birth certificate.
5. Me: Baristas could never afford that apartment! Her: I wanna be their black *Friend!*
6. Until the miniseries *Roots.* Then I felt shitty.

either. The last time I looked, we were in a war in the Middle East because a certain president was desperate not to be his.

Anyway, something good came out of those lost years: I wrote *The White Guy*, a one-man play that you might call the first draft of this book. It was seven monologues that basically explored the experience of life as a white guy, living in a white guy's world.

They were short monologues, and upbeat except for the parts about racial injustice, human history and Manitoba.

The White Guy ended up being produced by the Public Theater in New York, when the artistic director was George Wolfe, the most powerful non-white guy in American theatre, which led to the TV rights being purchased by Quincy Jones, a legendary non-white guy who produced, among other things, Michael Jackson's *Thriller* and *The Fresh Prince of Bel-Air*.

This book expands upon a theme I explored in the play, namely that being white and a guy is a racial experience, too. Because it is a book, and I don't have to cast it, I have expanded it from being the story of one white guy living in a white guy's world, to the story of the white guy's role in human history, and how he managed to stay above the title for three thousand years or so, from around about the sack of Troy to the most recent sack of Baghdad, give or take the seventh century—when the Muslim Caliphate was in charge—and the '70s, which, when you think about it, were just flat-out embarrassing for everyone (except the Montreal Canadiens, OPEC and KC and the Sunshine Band).

This is a field guide, in which I put on my cultural anthropologist's hat and look at what makes white guys tick. Think of it as a tell-all exposé, part memoir, part confessional, part apology to the rest of the planet. With a few recipes, some adventure travel, tips for the slacker parent, the odd sports rant and a little relationship how-to advice.

And lists, *bien sûr*. Because white guys love lists. To paraphrase the late General de Gaulle, who paraphrased the even later Louis XIV: lists, *c'est moi*. Lists are one of our lasting contributions to

Western culture, not to mention late-night television and NFL pre-game shows. In fact, I can feel one coming on right now.

Top Ten List of Lists

1. Letterman's List. The founding father of the comedy list who still does them better than anyone alive.
2. The *New York Times* Bestseller List. We wish.
3. *Forbes's* Richest People List. Can you say, Bill Gates, Warren Buffet, dozens of dotcom-real estate-oil sheiks—and Oprah?
4. *People's* 50 Sexiest People Alive List. The list trifecta would have to be making #2 (*Times* bestsellers), # 3 (*Forbes's* richest) and #4 (*People's* sexiest) all in one year.
5. Mr. Blackwell's Worst Dressed List. Question: who's Mr. Blackwell and how does he dress?
6. Top-Grossing Movies of the Weekend. Thanks for that, Mr. Spielberg.
7. Canada's Politest Cities. Did they think rating Canada's coldest cities was too obvious?
8. Peter King's Top 500 Players in the NFL. Fantasy football fodder for losers!
9. FDA's Food Pyramid. Was calling it a pyramid some sort of desperate attempt at diversity?
10. America's Most Wanted. Mostly, the world just wants America to go back home.

Pourquoi White Guys?

So why a field guide to white guys? We all know there are millions of books out there, about birds, indigenous cultures, the Zen of baseball, how to survive on $350 a day in Paris, not to mention sailing—as if we all sit around all day praying someone writes another book about *sailing*. You know, I've been sailing. It makes you nauseous, and all you do is run into other bored white guys out on the water, wondering if it's time to start drinking yet. Bet on it: there'll be lots of new books about sailing this spring, but the only book about white guys you'll be able to read in diverse company will be this one.[7]

The toughest thing about growing up white and a guy is that it's not so tough. Nothing ever happens to you. Living with your parents well into your thirties? One of those child soldiers in Sierra Leone ought to try that on for size. Running for public office—and being taken seriously? How sad. Got a nifty web startup you created in your college dorm with your roomies? It turns out to be Facebook.

Let's face it, for white guys, the world has pretty much always been our oyster, sitting there on a silver platter, paid for with the company credit card, waiting for us to slurp it up.

So what's the problem? One word: material. And another: authenticity.

The fact is it's a big, fat competitive book market out there. Everyone has a story to tell, and the worse the story, the better the read. This puts a *ton* of pressure on white guys, most of whom have lived lives of relative privilege, to come up with a story someone else will actually spend money to *read*. That's why guys like James Frey make up life stories that sound way *worse* than their lives actually are: no one wants to read the story of a guy with no problems.

The White Guy may not shake up the cultural anthropological community the way *Coming of Age in Samoa* did back in the '30s, but if there is a cultural anthropological community, I suggest they all scrap cultural anthropology and go see a band. (And don't tell anyone at the bar that you are a member of the cultural anthropological community—it's a big turnoff.)

While my journey doesn't involve any stays in rehab, nights in jail, sex with celebrities, Tuesdays with Morrie or stints in the army fighting unwinnable wars in dusty, dangerous corners of the planet, I will do my best to make shit up if it helps the thing sell.

---

7. The rest will be written by guys with websites you get injunctions against.

You've been warned.

But first, a word from non-white, non-guys everywhere.

Hint: the word starts with the letter W.

W People

Melanee is fond of making sweeping observations about the ways of white people. Listening to her and her family and her non-white, non-guy friends talk about white people is kind of a privilege, even when they get it—in my opinion—completely wrong.[8]

My mother-in-law, a former Democratic Party political operative who was largely responsible for Jimmy Carter winning Delaware on his way to becoming president in 1977, will sit at the kitchen table with Melanee and tell stories about "W People." That's us! W People!

They talk about W People with a mixture of affection, bafflement and wariness. As well as a bit of—how shall I put it?—irritation? Annoyance? Rising indignation?

Okay. How about... anger?

I know, I know—sounds like a *lot* of marriages.

W People are a constant source of fascination to non-white, non-guys. How we dress (badly). How we communicate (not too warmly, at least with non-white guys and gals). What we value (Winning! Being in charge! Walking quietly! Carrying a big stick!). Who we are attracted to (Blondes?). Who we invite into our inner sanctums, where all the best jobs, movie deals, columnist spots, insider stock deals, real estate steals and cabinet positions get divvied up.[9]

I have had years of significant exposure to the non-white, non-guy perspective on my species, and trust me, white people might

---

8. Like that theory floating around that white people originally came from outer space. We originally came from the Iowa Caucausus, an obscure province in Central Asia known for selecting presidential candidates.

9. Could someone please email the address of the inner sanctum? I seem to have lost it.

think we live in a world where colour no longer matters, but that's because we're W People living in a W Person's world, blissfully acting as if we're all living on the same colour-blind planet—the one where the weather's kind of crazy and no one can afford a house anymore, but hey, if you got into the market before prices went nuts, it's a beautiful place, isn't it?

The White Guy seeks to demonstrate that many of our most entrenched cultural beliefs—among them the denim shirt/khaki pants combo, secular humanism, mountain climbing, fun runs for charity and inordinate love of small ball and beer—are actually unique to white guys, and not representative of some larger, universal human truth.

Furthermore, the sooner white guys wake up and acknowledge there are other ways of looking at things besides our way—say, for example, yoga—the sooner we stop launching pre-emptive invasions of countries in order to assist them in embracing democratic "ideals."

Although *The White Guy* could always send some other message I'm not counting on. That's one of the more sizeable problems whenever the subject turns to race: you start out trying to say one thing, and you end up going on Larry King to say *sorry about that*, right before checking into rehab for a month in the country.

I HAVE AN IDEA. How about a pre-emptive apology?

After all, not only am I a white guy, I'm also Canadian. Isn't apologizing what a Canadian white guy does best? For pretty much all of our short history, we have walked behind American White Guy—and prior to that, British Empire White Guy—with the proverbial pooper scooper, a shovel and a hair-trigger willingness to say, "Sorry about that."

So, to everyone I have offended, I would like to offer my sincerest apologies. If I haven't offended you yet, just give it a few more pages.

Let's face it: we're all a little bit racist. Pretending we aren't is just giving us a bunch of sprained tongues. White guys have been closely associated with racism for hundreds of years now, but trust me, the tendency to make racial judgments about people doesn't begin and end with old, wrinkly ex-shock jocks like Don Imus.

Everyone makes racial judgements about everyone. In Los Angeles, Latinos make them about African-Americans. In Africa, Somalis make them about Kenyans. The Japanese make them about Koreans. The Germans, well, never mind. In France, the French make them about Belgians, Muslims, the British, the rural French and people from Quebec. They're so busy making racial judgments in France, they forgot to have an economy.

It's not pretty. It's not ideal. It's often horrible. It's just people being people. But has becoming hypersensitive about race really solved anything, or does it just create more problems?

James Fallows, a longtime *Atlantic Monthly* correspondent, once went to live in Japan. I still remember his first dispatch, in which he wrote about how it's ridiculous not to observe that there are differences between the Japanese and American cultures. The problems start, he wrote, when you try to determine what's better or worse.

I don't even think we mean it half the time when we show our racist fangs. I think we're all trying—in ways that are frequently awkward, ill-conceived or downright dumb—to have a conversation that's just as much about what's different between each of us as it is about what's better or worse. We just manage, quite frequently, to mangle our words—particularly white guys, who quite often don't appreciate that the baggage their words are dragging around would keep a jumbo jet from taking off.

In *The White Guy*, we take a closer look at some of the rituals of my people, hopefully to better understand such previously unexplored mysteries as the enduring popularity of South African *biltong* (jerky), German humour, Canadian passion, American open-mindedness, British dental hygiene, Australian subtlety,

Scandinavian brunettes and Russian understatement. We'll turn the microscope on white guy's cuisine, habitat, mating rituals, political systems, recreational pastimes, cars, technology, protection devices, mood-altering preferences and modes of dress.

Because, truth be told, not every white guy is the same. We just look the same, more or less, with Clooney on the high end and Cheney on the low.[10] But we're not the same. I swear. George W. Bush and I are both big baseball fans. I like a mixed drink. But the similarity ends there. Trust me. Really. I swear it's the truth.

Raise your hand if you've heard that one before.

. . . .

MEL'S DEEP THOUGHT

(The first in an occasional series of interruptions to the narrative flow)

No. I: THE MORE YOU TALK ABOUT RACISM, THE MORE THERE IS . . .

IF YOU, a person of colour, tell a well-meaning white friend that you've experienced racism, the well-meaning white friend has a flashback to all those times they were terrified some person of colour was going to 1) rape, 2) rob or 3) suicide-bomb them.

An immediate sense of guilt and shame descends upon the well-meaning white friend for all those lurking suspicions. So as not to feel like a horrible racist bastard, the well-meaning white friend immediately justifies his fears and suspicions by listing all the times he *was* justified.

Remember that newspaper headline, remember that mugging, remember that...

Then, the well-meaning white friend slowly begins to turn his guilt/suspicions onto you, a disgruntled person of colour, by pointing out your racially associated deficiencies: public displays of

---

10. Cheney might argue that novelist Stephen King is more ugly. This is like Wyoming arguing that it has prettier strip mines than Montana.

anger, lateness, issues regarding being disorganized. Thus well-meaning white friend gets into a dance of feeling accused, guilty, angry, suspicious—before he finally calms down by justifying his feelings of racism.

As a result, it is usually best not to talk about racism with white people. It's better to save your stories for those times when you are around other people of colour, when you can vent and express your bafflement at all the manoeuvring that surviving in a white world requires without sending the listener into some sort of racial shame spiral.

However, the flip side of this is that it leads to a kind of social schizophrenia: when you are with white friends, you feel like a liar and hypocrite at worst or, at best, one who suffers from multiple personality disorder. Especially if your best friend is your husband, who happens to be white.

End of Deep Thought.

. . . .

(Now you tell me!)

INTRODUCTION

WHITE GUYS: A CLOSER LOOK

. . .

ANYONE WHO ever watched a *National Geographic* special on Africa knows that each tribe is different. Some tribes feature guys who are tall; some feature guys who are short (but lethal with a blow dart). Some tribes speak entirely in clicks. Others spend their days wandering the desert in search of food, shade and Coca-Cola bottles falling from the sky.[1]

White guys are a loose collection of tribes featuring their own unique rituals, cuisine, habitat, political systems and modes of dress.[2] Some white guys are tall (highly electable); some are tiny (but good listeners). Some wander the desert in search of a miracle (also known as Middle Eastern democracy) and speak in

1. This from *The Gods Must Be Crazy*, which was an Australian movie, not a *National Geographic* special; but why quibble when we're talking about a place with no oil whatsoever?

2. The Professional Golfers' Association (PGA), grunge musicians and goths are but three examples. And Santa Monica mailmen, who deliver in khaki shorts.

incomplete sentences (see the collected speeches of the president of the United States). Others set up shop on the outskirts of villages (the suburbs), erecting temples to the family and filling them with plasma televisions, sports equipment and automobiles, then installing elaborate home protection devices that go off at inappropriate moments and annoy the hell out of the neighbours.

White guys have always been meticulous about record keeping, and you know what they say about who gets to write history: *what oral tradition? We've got it in writing, pal.*

Since white guys have written quite a bit of human history, we tended to come off pretty well, at least until the mid-'60s or so. Thanks to all those Vietnam draft dodgers who ended up getting faculty positions in Canada, the last forty years have been filled with dissenting voices, or, barring that, some highly dubious clothing combinations, a lot of sensible shoes and skyrocketing sales for acoustic-guitar-playing singer-songwriters. What seems to be missing from the discourse, however, is a comprehensive, objective, academic, thoroughly researched study of the various tribes of white guys and our rituals, beliefs and (property) values.

There won't be one when you reach the end of this book, either, but it will have to do. Come on, I mean, do you really want *statistics* that prove shit? Know who invented statistics? A white guy with a sailing ship, in about the sixteenth century, trying to talk someone with money into financing his next road trip across the ocean. You can get statistics to prove anything.[3]

Living, as we do, in a high-strung, conflict-strewn planet filled with "evil villains" who seek to harm truth tellers and believers in justice and democracy, it just seems to be a good moment to do a quick fact check on this perspective on the world. After all, when you live at a time of religious war, nuclear proliferation and

---

3. Ever read one of those stories about how we have inflation tamed and wonder what planet statisticians live on, and how hard it is to qualify for a mortgage there?

climate change, getting it wrong could be the final mistake you get to make.[4]

Question: Who dropped not one but two nukes, killing several hundred thousand non-white guys? Who launched one of the most enduring religious crusades of all time? Who has done way, way more than their share of eroding the ozone layer?

Answer: Are you warming to my theme yet?

That said, quite often these missteps were taken with the very best of intentions. After all, World War II had to end somehow. Possibly, Pope Urban II overreacted, but that was back in 1095, well before CNN and the Internet, and the Turks did have pretty scary curved swords. And sure the ozone is shot to hell, but because of that, I'm sitting in a nice, comfy house at the end of February, writing a book, instead of out foraging on the ice, wrapped in bearskin, searching for something to kill for breakfast. It is easy to sit back in a chair from the comfy perspective of the early twenty-first century and rewrite the first three thousand years just to wring some cheap laughs out of history.

Now that you mention it, I think I will.

Why Me?

Excellent question. After all, white guys are quite the demographic, aren't we? We're about 75 per cent of the Fortune 500, every Pope, and every former U.S. president. If white guys need someone to speak for them, why don't we get Bill Clinton? Well, his wife is running for president, for one thing. Or Warren Beatty? He's not doing much—and don't think he doesn't die a little every time Clint Eastwood collects another award, making him the artsy seventy-something of the moment. Bill Gates? Too busy giving away billions. Warren Buffett? Too busy earning them. Don

---

4. Like who gets to have nukes, and who doesn't? Who wrote that rulebook? Did I miss it? Is it like the no-tuck rule in the NFL?

Cherry? Haven't we all had about enough Don Cherry? David Beckham? Now that England failed again at the World Cup in 2006, what's Becks doing with the rest of his life, besides shopping with Posh in between photo shoots for his latest skin care product?[5] John Updike? Is anyone whiter than John Updike?[6]

Why me?

Well, why not? I am white. I am a guy. Hear me self-deprecate.

(Al Gore was asked to do it, but he makes too much money flying around doing that slide show about how the airline industry is killing the planet.)

Is This Really Necessary?

The other question you might have rattling around in your dome is, why write about white guys at all? What's the *point*? Isn't any discussion of white guys bound to end up somewhere uncomfortable? Unpleasant, even? If you don't offend non-white guys, non-guys and the Danish, then you're bound to end up pissing off white guys who hate it when anyone suggests they got what they got at least in part because they're white and they're guys.

Why go *there*?

Excellent question.

Don't you think it's about time we studied ourselves? Non-white guys and non-guys have been studying us for years,[7] mostly because if they didn't do their homework, there was always the chance they'd get shot in the back by accident by the cops, imported to work for free or, these days, put on a midnight flight to Syria for a year of waterboarding and testicular electrolysis. Ask any non-white guy about white people. He'll know more about us than we could ever imagine—way more than we know about ourselves.

---

5. Becks moved to L.A. Sooner or later, everyone does.
6. Tom Hanks is whiter than John Updike. Ask anyone.
7. See *The Women's Room, The Feminine Mystique* and *He's Just Not That Into You.*

Now there's even a non-white guy television network: Al-Jazeera.

We're not about rewriting history in *The White Guy*. We're about apologizing for it.

"Sorry" really is the hardest word. *The White Guy* is here to say it![8]

The White Guy: A Definition-in-Progress

The white guy of the eleventh century was not the same white guy you see crossing the street in his Crocs today. Ten centuries ago, Anglos wore out their swords battling Saxons. Now they're the same word. Go figure.

Who, exactly, is a white guy and who is not? For example, when we say white guy, I think we can all agree that we are talking about a guy who is white. But beyond that, things get tricky. Truth is, being a white guy is more a state of mind than a state of the union or a set of inherited genetic traits, which was the old-school way of determining these things before MySpace and Facebook made self-definition less a matter of genes and more about who has the most friends.[9]

Concepts like "guys" and "white" have become increasingly blurred, to the point where we're never going to be able to put anyone back in a genetic box and tie a bow around it. The world is rapidly becoming Brazil: a genetic mixed bag, without, alas, Brazilian butts or thong-friendly weather (although give the depleting ozone another five, six years and that could all change).

Are Spanish guys white guys? How about the guys from the Stan countries, like Borat? My mom is Ukrainian, and growing up in Western Canada in the '50s, Ukrainians were pretty much considered non-white guys, or at least not upper management material,

---

8. *The White Guy* also seeks to restore the reputation of the exclamation mark.

9. Those pesky genetic circumstances are the source of plenty of human misery, aren't they?

the same way Irish and Italians were viewed in places like New York, Boston and Chicago. But all of that changed, whether the gene pool vigilantes out there wanted it to or not.

Are gay guys who are white also *white guys?* How about Jewish guys? How can you have spent centuries being persecuted by a group and also be part of it?

If this trend continues, sooner or later we will all be white guys. Either that, or none of us will be. Imagine that: a world where the white guy is extinct, gone the way of T. Rex, the drugstore soda fountain and afternoon World Series games.

That's why the 2008 U.S. presidential election is so much fun. The country finally saw what a bunch of white guys sitting around in their corner offices in Washington could do to the world—absolutely wreck it—and they came to their senses. Whether they elect a non-guy, a non-white guy or Ralph Nader, all I know is that Americans seem about ready to hand over the keys to the country to the first non-white guy or non-guy President. It's about time, too.

It seems to me that defining the white guy has echoes of that judge who was asked to define pornography. You can't exactly put it into words, but you know it when you see it.

Until then, for all of you non-white guys and non-guys out there: take out your notebooks and pencils, for I am about to reveal the secret, inner life of white guys everywhere.

Welcome to the inner sanctum. I'll need a name, email address, credit card number and expiry date, please.

For all of you white guys, people like me, I'll meet you at the appointed time and place, to go over the list of who gets into heaven and who doesn't. You'll know me by the secret handshake.

This is my world. Welcome.

CLOTHES

— *or* —

PLUMAGE

. . .

THE WHITE GUY may be universally recognized for his penchant for hogging all the good jobs, being in charge and living a commitment to excellence, but he is also acknowledged to be a fashion disaster.

"You can walk around, dressed like butt, and nobody cares," Melanee says one day, in the one-bedroom apartment where we lived in Santa Monica for nine years. "I have to get dressed up before I go out, or people in this rich, pseudo-liberal neighbourhood think I'm some kind of crazy homeless chick."

I never heard the term "dressed like butt" before Melanee used it, but it has the ring of truth to it.

Why do white guys dress like butt?

That's complicated.

Perhaps we should make like a good homicide cop, and analyze our motivation. Once you understand motivation, all the fashion atrocities white guys commit fall neatly into place.

Let us review then, a few of the fatal psychological errors white guys make when deciding what to wear every single day all over the world:

1. There's another year left in this suit. (There isn't. There hasn't been for half a decade.)
2. No one cares what you wear on Saturdays. (We do.)
3. There's no need to wear a suit on opening night. I'll just wear this colourful *(read: awful)* sweater instead. It goes with every pair of pants I own. (It goes with nothing.)
4. I'm driving after work, so I need to wear something comfortable. (After work is your business. We have to look at you dressed like a homeless person until 5:30.)
5. This is my good luck shirt. (From 1977.)
6. The team has good luck whenever I wear this jersey. (Okay. Maybe there's something to that.)
7. The layered look works on me. (You're a man, not a cake.)
8. You can't see the stain on these pants. (Yes, you can see the stain.)
9. I hardly did anything when I wore this stuff yesterday. I can squeeze another day out of them. (Guilty.)
10. I'm always online. Who cares what I'm wearing? (You make baristas want to scream.)

These sorts of psychological presumptions have produced generation after generation of sartorial disasters, often committed by highly successful guys, the leaders of the free world.
Result:

Ten White Guys Who Dress Like Butt

10. Nick Nolte, actor. Perhaps Nick's problem is that he keeps getting arrested on his worst-dressed days. Just a guess.
9. Stephen Harper, Canadian prime minister. Has mastered the look that says, "I'm the doughy little brother who always sucked

at sports but did really good at school and now I'm the Canadian prime minister with a hot wife! Hand me that leather vest!"

8. Craig Sager, TNT sports analyst. Worst suits ever. His personal style icon: The Joker.

7. Don Imus, American radio personality. They say some are born with a face for radio (check). How about a wardrobe that looks like a Cody, Wyoming, wax museum come to life?

6. (tie) Kevin Smith, film director and Michael Moore, documentary film maker. Comic book geek and indie film icon; overweight Jersey guy. Left-wing man-of-the-people with a fondness for flannel that should have died the day Kurt Cobain did. Someone needs to do a reality show about these two getting dressed in the morning.

5. Sporty, West Coast Athletic White Guy. During the week, you're stuck in a suit. On the weekend, you put on your cycling/kayaking/jogging/rock climbing/skiing/mountaineering/parasailing/hiking gear, which involves most of the United Colors of Benetton, all at the same time in a skin-tight, waterproof superhero outfit. Who decided this was okay? I want a recount!

4. Don Cherry, *Hockey Night in Canada* icon. Something has gone very, very wrong with this man's wardrobe.

3. Bill Belichick, head coach, New England Patriots. Someone take that hooded sweatshirt out back and shoot it.

2. Bill Gates. Our finest living testament to Geek Classicism.

1. Stephen King, novelist, Red Sox fan. I have two words: eyebrow trimmer.

Forgive Me My Daily Dress

The other day, Mel brought me home new shorts from the mall. Shorts are a source of irritation for her. Shorts are one of those things white guys wear in almost any situation, no matter how stupid it makes them look. We seem to have adopted the philosophy that when the temperature reaches a certain point—say, 65°F—it is our constitutional right, as white guys raised in winter climates, to wear short pants that make us look like schoolboys in middle-aged bodies.

The best example of this philosophy has always been Bermuda White Guy, who combines the suit jacket and dress shoes with the khaki shorts, a look which recalls Angus of the Aussie band AC/DC—a look I've always found kind of compelling, even if is sort of the mullet haircut of clothes.

So we win a pair of $75 gift certificates from the local mall at a work function. I give them to Melanee and send her off, ecstatic, to the mall, to blow the whole $150.

In order not to feel totally selfish and self-absorbed, she brings me home two pairs of shorts, but they aren't quite my style of Old Navy, side-pockety, Bermuda White Guy shorts. They're a little shorter than that. They have slash pockets. And on the butt pockets, there are *flaps*.

Furthermore, instead of that camping kind of khaki, they're a little thin, a little more citified than I like my shorts to be—because, basically, for the first four decades of my life, I've been good with hacking the legs off a pair of pants and calling them shorts.

But I don't want to cause a problem.

"I like them," I say. But I don't wear them.

A few days later, she wants to take some stuff back to the mall. She hasn't really bought anything that knocks her out, mostly because $150 doesn't get you much at the mall these days, particularly when you have to spread it around. At the moment, there is only $12 left on the card, and she needs some item of clothing for a play she's doing.

"Tell you what," I say. "Take the shorts back and use the extra dough to buy your wardrobe thing." I'm hoping she will overlook the fact that I'm rejecting her shorts and embrace the fact that this will boost the value of the card by $40 or so.

Fat chance.

"You don't like those shorts?"

"They're fine. But that's a lot to spend on shorts."

"You think they're gay, don't you?"

I pause. How to put it? After all, what's wrong with looking gay? Gay guys dress better than I ever will. It's just the little voice that lives inside of me, the white guy who is constantly trying to wring one more day out of that T-shirt, or to dress down for a company function because you're really more comfortable dressing like that—well, yeah. You're more comfortable when you dress like butt—and it shows!

And even though I know Mel is better at clothes than I am— she just is—I can't get the little voice to shut its yap.

"They're a little too Stedman for me," I say, referring to Oprah's somewhat over-suave fiancé.

She shakes her head sadly. You can almost see the little thought bubble form over her pretty little head:

White guys dress like such dorks!

Not all white guys dress like butt. Plumage depends to a large extent on climate, region and cultural sensibility, as any competent bird watcher knows. Likewise, white guy plumage varies from currency to currency, continent to continent and industry to industry.

British white guys wear the best suits on the planet, or maybe they just have the best posture. French Photojournalist White Guy on assignment in Iraq manages to be dusty, dirty and yet perfectly elegant. German Architect White Guy can do more with a simple pair of eyeglasses than most of us could ever dream of: make eyeglasses seem cool.

However, North American White Guy, as a rule, dresses like butt.

Melanee is not only a non-white, non-guy, but she is an actor,[1] so she takes great care to dress well. She is a great shopper for clothes, someone who can spot the perfect item in a pile at the Goodwill for $2. Women frequently stopped her in Santa Monica to ask where she got what she was wearing, despite the fact that

---

1. Someone addicted to the opinions of others.

what she was wearing generally didn't cost $20 and what they were wearing cost hundreds and hundreds of dollars.

Anyway, Melanee isn't the only one who thinks North American White Guy dresses like butt. So, apparently, does Elton John.

Sir Elton recently ripped American musicians, whom he said didn't care what they wore, or even worse, relied upon the tattoo-and-piercings look for an image, which he hates. According to Sir Elton, British acts such as he (!!) were much better when it came to clothes. Here's what he said in an interview with *Fashion Rocks* magazine:

It's been a thing the British have always been very good at, with Bowie, myself, T. Rex, The Who, Queen ... We all embraced that side of it. And I think it's good that some American bands are beginning to do that, but it's still very rare for bands to make a real effort. So when you get groups like The Killers and Scissor Sisters who come along, it's thrilling. I'm so over the tattoos and the T-shirts and rings through the noses. It's not pretty, it's not pleasant, it's not exciting. Please stop it now.

The problem is that the white guy dresses for other white guys. We want to be liked (by guys) just as much as we want to be loved (by women), and somewhere along the way, someone drew up a white guy dress code that stated that none of us will appear to try too hard. None of us will try to be too pretty, in case we discover we are attracted to each other. And when in doubt, a team jersey is perfectly appropriate.

Now that we live in Calgary, rather than Hollywood or New York, the plumage of the local white guy has gotten even worse.

"Why do white men constantly dress like shit?" Mel asks. "You can have a good-looking white man, but the brother can't dress himself. It's okay for black men to be pretty, same with Latino men. Why do all y'all white guys dress so bad?"

Why ask why? We just do. It's part of our charm. And no, I have no plans to tuck this shirt in.

One White Guy Who Doesn't Dress Like Butt

Rufus Wainwright is a rock star. In fact, he's sort of the Elton John of the twenty-first century. He writes catchy, smart songs, and he's gay.

Rufus went on CBC Radio and did all white guys a huge favour. He made a list of five things every guy should own (to keep him from dressing like butt).

Rufus Wainwright's Five Things Every Guy Should Own

1. A necklace. According to Rufus, the shinier, the better.
2. Jeans that make your butt look cute. Well, every guy wants his butt to look cute. Come on.
3. Converse sneakers. And don't be afraid to make them boldly hued Converse sneakers! (Only wear for social purposes and not actual vigorous walking, as they don't have any arch support.)
4. An expensive white shirt. White shirts show their price tags.
5. A really cool, old T-shirt. Or possibly, a really *new*, semi-expensive vintage T-shirt that looks old, minus the sweat-stained pits and salsa splotches that my bona fide old T-shirts all have.

How People Dress in Vancouver

"I know it's the most beautiful city on the planet or whatever," Mel says as we walk down Denman Street one summer day, almost apologetically. "But I just can't get into this place. People in Vancouver wear way too much fleece."

Ten Common White Guy Plumage Don'ts

10. Overreliance on sports socks. Guilty.
9. Sports jacket worn with jeans. Is this a look, or a cry that you're conflicted?
8. Denim shirt/khaki pants combo. The team uni for Middle Management White Guy. Maybe it's time to try a throwback jersey or something.

7. Torn-jeans-wearing young celebrities. I tore my jeans, and I wore them, and trust me, Mr. Ashton Federline-Timberlake-Whatever, you don't know from torn jeans.

6. The white-collar-baby-blue-dress-shirt-yellow-power-tie-Wall-Street-circa-1987 look. Throw it out and buy a pink dress shirt and tell all your friends to buy this book.

5. Von Dutch trucker hats. Are so 2002! Related: chains on wallets. Okay, you're a killer. I'm impressed. Just don't get hooked by the garbage truck as he empties the dumpster in your back alley.

4. Pressed jeans. How very un-casual Friday.

3. Workout clothes as casual wear. Try a little harder, would ya? And mix in a shower.

2. The sweater vest. Nothing says non-threatening, sexless, yes-man quite so effortlessly. The question is, why?

1. Wearing sneakers all the time. I know they're comfortable. I know you're not trying to impress anyone. You're doing an excellent job of that.

Chapter Summary

The white guy dresses for other white guys, or, to put it more bluntly, like butt. And that's okay.

CUISINE OF THE
WHITE MALE

. . .

PEOPLE ON THE Indian subcontinent favour cur-
ried vegetables and lentils. Asia is dominated
by rice, the dietary staple of half the world's population. Whole
swathes of Africa feature cuisine based around the joys of the sweet
potato. White guys like them all—and meat. Lots and lots and lots
of meat. Sure, it clogs your heart. Yes, all of those grazing, farting
cows warm an already unseasonably hot planet. No one likes to
think about those melancholy, soon-to-be-beheaded chickens living cheek by jowl (fowl?) in some industrial park in the American
Midwest, awaiting their afterlife as chicken nuggets shaped like
characters from *Toy Story*.

There are different degrees of this rule—it varies according to
geography, income, education and whether or not you are the type
of white guy who likes to train for triathlons or kayak across the
Georgia Strait in windstorms—but all white guys are variations on

the same theme: we love to eat meat! Even Vegetarian White Guy likes meat—he just thinks not eating what he likes makes him morally superior to the rest of us. (It might.)

The Joy of Burgers

Unlike with television (invented by a white guy) or the personal computer (again), no one is quite sure who invented the hamburger, although the consensus is that it was an American white guy.

Texans claim that a Texan named Fletcher Davis invented the burger in the 1880s, serving them to great acclaim to all those Texas Rangers who would eventually be played on television mini-series by the likes of Robert Duvall and Tommy Lee Jones. In 1904, Davis made the trek to the World's Fair in St. Louis, set up a burger stand, and was immediately joined by another guy selling French-fried potatoes. Instant chemistry.

But Connecticut Yankees have a counter-claim. They say Louis Lassen of New Haven served the first burgers in 1900, as a kind of new-millennium treat for all of those Yale white guy freshmen just arrived in town, oblivious that the twentieth century was theirs to ruin.

Lassen served burgers—on toast, with cheese, tomatoes and onions—at Louis Lunch, and unbelievably, Louis Lunch is still there, still serving burgers to Yale freshmen wondering if they're going to grow up to be president, or just Stephen Colbert.

Eating a good burger is a sensual experience, right up there with watching Angelina Jolie address the UN. It's erotic-gastronomic. If it's medium rare, with some Dijon mustard, ketchup, onions, tomato, lettuce, pepper, salt, a dab of mayo all ladled onto a lightly toasted sesame bun, it can't get much better than that.

Almost every place you go in North America, you will find a memorable burger. They are one of the few great things that are still accessible to almost anyone. Most of us will never know the pleasures of Kobe beef, or drink wine older than the fruit in the back of the fridge. We can only dream of winning the lottery so we can afford tickets to the Super Bowl or World Series. We saw Paris, before the Euro went nuts; now we recall it, in a kind of fond haze, like a beautiful ex-girlfriend who only wanted to be friends.

But if you have twenty bucks, you can still sample a fine burger, often at some modest, no-nonsense diner. In New York, the Corner Bistro in the West Village serves mugs of draft beer, has the ambiance of a student pub and serves sublime cheeseburgers. In California, In-N-Out Burger makes the most legendary burgers of any fast food franchise, which is only fitting, because what is California's contribution to the culture, if not the drive-through, fast food, cholesterol orgy that is the burger, fries and shake?

The Rise and Fall of Beef

In recent decades, beef has suffered tremendously in the meat PR department, reversing a decades-long trend where beef reigned supreme on the white guy menu. Beef was the New York Yankees, the Montreal Canadiens and the All Blacks all rolled into one. Gangsters, politicians, movie stars and athletes all worshipped at the altar of the steakhouse. Humphrey Bogart may have said it best: "Nothing beats roast beef at the Ritz."

I loved Humphrey Bogart. He was like a hard-boiled, cigarette-smoking Clooney.

Somehow, though, around 1980, chicken and fish got the upper hand, mainly because some chicken publicist got their hands on some statistics linking heart disease to beef consumption or some other nutritional insight like that. I'm not going to engage in a debate about the healthfulness of various types of meat. I mean, I'm like everybody—opting for the chicken or fish, unless I start loathing my reflexive goody two-shoes behaviour, at which point I select the beef. I also have a lifetime love affair going with bacon. Bacon ranks right up there with day games at Yankee Stadium as a personal pleasure for me, and I don't care if the National Institutes of Health publishes a Russian novel about how eating bacon contributes to the rise of terrorism around the world. I'm still eating it.

Meat around the World

1. *Biltong* (beef jerky). South African White Guy is a sucker for jerky, which is chewy and salty and pure meat, and can travel in heat · without going off. North American Trucker White Guy likes it too.

2. Bangers. British Pub-Dwelling White Guy eats these sausages with his mash(-ed potatoes). Bangers and mash are the hard-boiled eggs of England: the last resort meal to give a drunk a little nutrition.

3. Dodger dogs. What you get at Dodger Stadium, which for about fifty years has been close to the penultimate baseball going experience. I hate Aramark, the Dodgers' concessionaire, but given that, if you catch a grilled Dodger dog on the right weeknight, on a year the Dodgers have an offence, it can be a sublime experience.

4. Cheeseburger medium rare. My friend Kevin Patterson gets the nod for the single most erotic burger ever eaten. It was after he single-handedly solo-sailed a thirty-five-foot cement-hulled boat called *The Sea Mouse* from Tahiti to B.C. By the end of the trip, he was punchy, hallucinating, living on tins of crap and some vodka and pornography a Russian fishing boat had given him. By the time he docked *The Sea Mouse* somewhere on the northern tip of Vancouver Island, he hadn't washed in weeks and had a long beard, like a hermit or Alexander Solzhenitsyn. The first thing he did, before he even checked into a motel and grabbed a shower, was to hit the pub for a pint and a burger.[1] I can't imagine there was ever a finer meal consumed.

5. Bacon. Every Larry McMurtry novel about the Old West is full of lonely, grubby, emotionally inarticulate cowboys travelling long distances across the West. This is cool and romantic enough, but at night, when they start a campfire and cook dinner, it invariably involves bacon eaten under the stars by sad, lonely guys longing for something. Reading a few McMurtry cookout scenes makes you run, salivating, to the Safeway meat department.

---

1. Read about it in his excellent sailing memoir, *The Water in Between*.

6. Steak-frites. French White Guy likes to mock, of course, and has the good hair and high cheekbones to get away with it. When it comes to cheeseburgers and fries, the French sniff, but offer French White Guy a good steak-frites to go with his glass of Cabernet and chances are, he'll jump. (Likewise those pseudo-francophilian New Yorkers who are really just meat-eating white guys craving steak-frites at one of the dozens of imitation French restaurants that charge you a small fortune to pretend you're dining in the Marais rather than on West Broadway.)

The Eating Habits of Coastal White Guy

Food is a great equalizer. Preparing food is a wonderful skill to learn. Of all the life skills a guy can learn, knowing how to fix dinner is one that is a lock to keep you around if you're in a relationship. Knowing how to prepare food is sort of the life equivalent to playing good defence if you're a basketball player: it's not glamorous. It's not a mid-six-figure salary, or a nice expense account, or porn star–style lovemaking technique. But people gotta eat.

There are white guys who eat no meat. Some of them don't eat cooked food. Some of them only eat local food, organic food or food that they buy at Whole Foods, a sexy grocery chain that people in my former Santa Monica neighbourhood—the non-millionaires—referred to as Whole Paycheque.

In fact, food has become the final frontier for class distinction in the twenty-first century. It used to be that the rich owned the car, the television or the monstrously oversized house, but as time has gone on, all of these have become accessible for just about anyone. Even people in the ghetto have gorgeous flat screen plasma televisions and tricked-out rides with DVD players and GPS instrumentation that would make an airline weep. The real class distinctions these days are what and where you eat.

Of course, just as there was the odd vegetarian dinosaur roaming the plains during the Cretaceous Period lecturing T. Rex about what he put inside his body, so too is there a strain of white guy who does not build his cuisine upon slabs of grilled flesh. This tends to be a certain strain of Coastal White Guy. He is a high-achieving guy determined to remain at his college weight all his life. He moisturizes. He works out. He only dates hard bodies. He only ingests the best of whatever it is he ingests.

This brand of white guy orders sushi à la carte. He frequents raw food restaurants. He's all about excellence, or maximizing himself, or maximizing you. He sends things back to the kitchen with alarming regularity. He spends way more than any self-respecting guy ought to spend on a haircut. Yes, he's L.A. White Guy—only L.A. White Guy has spread his wings and now may live in your city, whether that city is New York, Boston, Washington, Sydney, Stockholm, Reykjavík, London or Capetown. He's a strain of white man known as the metrosexual, the first-ever demographic group of guys who love shopping for something other than a ride. (For more on this unusual subspecies, see Interlude B: The Pursuit of Excellence vs. The New Mediocrity.)

Doesn't Cook White Guy

There is a hamburger chain in California called Carl's Jr. that has been running a series of commercials for a while now. They usually feature a twentysomething white guy—the semi-unemployed variety—tentatively making his way through the aisles of his local grocery store, a look of abject despair on his face as he contemplates the horror, the horror—the thought of preparing his own dinner.

Cut to the guy sitting in a Carl's Jr., chowing down on one of their massive, mediocre burgers. The tagline: "Without us, some guys would starve."

Meet Doesn't Cook White Guy.

Doesn't Cook White Guy isn't a bad guy. He isn't stupid, undereducated, sexually inadequate or a geek.

He just can't cook.

Doesn't Cook White Guy is one of those sad stories, like the one about the secretly illiterate guy who has been faking it for all these years when it comes time to read the handouts at school. Doesn't Cook White Guy has gotten by on Mom, the school cafeteria, camp kitchen, room service, takeout and the taco stand and the drive thru and—*horrors*—the hot dog grill at the AM/PM for years. One day he wakes up, remembers he's thirty-two, hung over and, *holy shit*—

He forgot to learn how to cook.

It isn't as if Doesn't Cook White Guy hasn't tried. There have been mishaps with omelettes, marinara massacres, grilling grotesqueries and horror shows involving lasagna. All of it usually involved a female, because Doesn't Cook White Guy heard that chicks dig Guys Who Cook and he had the epiphany that the reason his life was such an unfulfilled void was because he doesn't cook.

Unfortunately, Doesn't Cook White Guy doesn't cook for a good reason: he's terrible at it.

It isn't the end of the world to be Doesn't Cook White Guy. Some white guys in fact probably assume it to be a sign of the highest status to be Doesn't Cook White Guy. They have so many more important things to do than cook! Who has time?

Of course, every meal is not a sonnet when you are Doesn't Cook White Guy. There are moments when you find yourself absolutely starving in the apartment and unable, for one reason or another, to obtain outside food.

That's when things can get ugly.

Five Staples of Doesn't Cook White Guy

1. Cold cereal. Honey Nut Cheerios go down well whether they are garnished with milk or eaten raw, in the vegan style, and provide an oddly compelling buzz when eaten in combination with beer.
2. Canned soup. Although some find it perturbing that canned soup is made of seemingly indestructible ingredients all slammed together in a can that's been sitting on a shelf for half a decade, I

do not. I am a big fan of canned soup. How does canned soup do it? How does it keep from going bad? What could be in there that makes it taste so good, apart from enough salt to seize the heart of the most physically fit twenty-year-old on the block? Who cares? Now I'm full.

3. Unidentified sandwich meat. Sandwich meat is a key element in every white guy's life, a process of discovery, a journey inside yourself, a voyage to the bottom of your small intestine. Ultimately, it's a pleasure cruise. For a long time, you might try to vary your sandwich meat, as if that were the key to producing a more well-rounded personality. However, at the end of the day, sandwich meat is pretty much sandwich meat. Sandwich meat—to paraphrase Mickey Rourke paraphrasing Charles Bukowski in *Barfly*—is *fuel*. Does anyone ask what kind of sandwich meat the Google guys eat? No, they do not. Those guys invented Google.

4. Leftover pizza. Pizza places often try to trigger business on the off-nights by offering two-fers and things like free sodas to inspire brand loyalty from pizza buyers. Domino's has been offering two pizzas for one on Tuesday nights for years. Yes, the chances that there is leftover pizza somewhere in the fridge are excellent. After all, isn't that what the narrow shelves, the ones you can't stand a beer up on, are for?

5. Vegetables. Eating your vegetables is always an issue when you're Doesn't Cook White Guy, because vegetables are tricky. Vegetables are frequently at the bottom of the priority list, unless you get some on your pizza, so Doesn't Cook White Guy compensates for this—in his own addled mind—by, every once in a while, purchasing a bag of baby carrots or one of those takeout containers of crudités they sell at the Safeway deli counter, together with the small tub of ranch dressing. You know: carrot sticks, a few sliced peppers, a baby tomato or two, a broccoli crown. Doesn't Cook White Guy buys these and figures that about balances things out. Of course, sometimes, the crudités get lost amidst the beer

and pizza and unidentified sandwich meat, and weeks go by, so squeeze before you bite. If the vegetable feels squishy, it is probably best just to abandon your plan and go with the takeout pizza, fistful of Honey Nut Cheerios—and a beer.

Feeding All White Guys: Two Tips

We're not saying food is crucial to long-term relationships, but how to put it?

Food is the sex of marriage.

So put away that Victoria's Secret catalogue, and pull out this chapter.

Above all else, white guys treasure two things in their grub: portion size and authenticity.

Portion size sounds kind of grotesque and base, probably because it is. But a guy is expected to buy the dinner on a date, right? White guys go through life picking up the cheque. That's what we're there for—we're the ones who have no reason not to be doing well, so we can pick up the cheque. And even if we're not doing so hot, we'll pick it up just to make things look good. So, is it too much to ask for a plate of food that makes a guy full?

I think not.

It makes guys happy, too. I know that in a metrosexual, low-fat, carbohydrate-averse society like the one many white guys now live in, this seems counter-intuitive, but just ask the burger chains about how popular their huge, disgusting portions are among guys. Their breakfast burritos made of about half a pound of melted cheese and six eggs and some turkey sausage, or their half-pound burgers smothered in chili cheese and mayonnaise—guys love 'em!

As for authenticity, white guys enjoy nothing more than discovering a new variety of ethnic cuisine no other white guy has ever eaten before. For decades now, W People have been trawling the ethnic neighbourhoods of their cities, anxiously scuffling off to various obscure corners of the globe and enrolling in cooking classes all in the name of learning about how to cook authentic, ethnic, non–W People food.

You've done it, haven't you? Come on. Admit it. I know it all seems a little trite now, but remember when everyone didn't eat sushi? That first heady rush you got chomping into one of those red chili peppers at your first Thai restaurant? The joy of just dropping into one of the Vietnamese restaurants on Spadina Avenue in Toronto, where some of the best Asian cooking in the world is there for any old W Person who can ride the streetcar over to sample?

Authentic New York

One night in New York in 1990 or so, while searching for a cheap feed with friends in town visiting from Canada, we came across a Tibetan restaurant—of all the obscure cuisines—on Second Avenue in the East Village. We ate some Tibetan cuisine (forgettable, sadly—maybe it needs to be eaten at high altitude), drank some Tibetan lager (Molson's is tastier, alas; maybe it needs to be drunk alone, in a monastery) and—the *coup de grâce*—seated at the table next to us was Beat poet Allen Ginsberg! We acted really cool and never said hi or anything because we wanted to seem like jaded New Yorkers instead of provincial Canadians who were experiencing the simultaneous thrill of authentic (albeit a little lame and overpriced) ethnic cuisine, in the legendary (but rapidly gentrifying) East Village, all in the proximity of a literary legend.

Being authentic is exhausting, particularly in a world that works harder every day to make one place look as much like the next. Shanghai, from what I hear, is filled with Starbucks outlets. Who needs that twelve-hour flight? You can be more authentic staying home and ordering takeout.

Three-Star White Guy

On the other side of the equation, white guys have always been the top chefs, the guys with the Michelin three stars, the guys whose names New Yorkers drop as if they were movie stars—"I dated Gray Kunz a few times, yeah.[2] David Bouley's kid goes to my pre-school."

Now, with the Food Network and a few other channels you might be vaguely aware of, Chef White Guy has even become a celebrity—although the qualities that make a guy a TV chef are not always cooking-related. (Like everything on television, it matters more if you're cute and funny, which really cuts into the supply of TV-friendly chefs.)

Oh, and be forewarned: if you just happen to make the acquaintance of some scrawny, pale, hollow-eyed, lip-biting, holistic, anti-war, vegan white guy who is allergic to everything except his toenails and strong black fair trade coffee, you are looking at thirty-five years of hell trying to get an edible meal on the table. He might be the next great genius. He might be really principled, and idealistic, and environmentally aware. He's also a high maintenance nightmare. Pass on this guy.

Chapter Summary

White guys still hunt and gather, although many prefer to order in.

---

2. He is a chef who once got four stars in the *New York Times*. My ex-girlfriend dated him. Talk about ratcheting up the stakes when you have to fix a little lunch on Saturday afternoon!

MOOD-ALTERING
SUBSTANCES

. . .

THE WHITE GUY has always been a fan of mood-altering substances. After all, life is just one day after another, and you never knew, back in the day, which day might be your last. There was plague, pestilence, Huns, Romans, the whims of the Pope, the King, the King's sadistic little brother who was angry and bitter because he'd never be the King and wanted a serf to take it out on, the Dark Ages, the rise of the British Empire, the tax collector, cholera, the collapse of the tulip bubble, the American Revolution, the potato famine, the end of slavery, the Civil War, the Boer War, the Wright Brothers inventing flight, World War I, the dead ball era, the Communist Revolution, the Great Depression, the New Deal, the birth of jazz, World War II, suburbs, Arthur Miller plays, Rock Hudson romantic comedies, the rise of the American Empire, IBM, I Like Ike, the McCarthy Witch Hunt, JFK, the Bay of Pigs, the Summer of Love, Vietnam, OPEC, Stagflation, the Carter administration, Reagan, the Falklands War, the stock boom, AIDS, the rise of the Bush Dynasty, the fall of the Berlin Wall, *Goodfellas*, Scott Norwood wide right, the first Gulf War, the death of Kurt Cobain, the rave scene, the end of Apartheid, the rise of Bubba, Rwanda, Kosovo, Monica, New Labour and Britney, the stolen 2000 election, the bursting of the dotcom bubble, 9/11, the housing boom, Iraq, the bursting of the housing bubble. And we haven't even gotten to Al Gore winning the Nobel Peace Prize. Life has been fraught with peril, brimming with joy or simply a little dull ever since there's been life.

To paraphrase Kermit the Frog, it's not easy being white (and a guy). Okay, it's not that it's not easy—it's just hard waking up every day, looking around at the state of the world, and knowing you have no one to blame but yourself. I guess that's what Rudyard Kipling meant when he coined the phrase "the White Man's Burden."[1]

We prefer to call it "Happy Hour."

The form of mood alteration the white guy prefers depends on the local culture and the decade, but it's safe to say there are a few universal substances white guys the world around have been enjoying for ten or twenty centuries, and figure to still be enjoying long after the ozone is gone and everyone lives in geodesic domes filled with theme bars offering a generous array of cocktails invented in countries that are now completely underwater.

Would you like your tsunami on ice or blended, sir?

Brewskis and Other Beverages

Beer is popular nearly everywhere white guys gather, give or take the Napa Valley and Lynchburg, Tennessee. NASCAR Fan White Guy—particularly the one standing on the infield since ten in the morning on race day with little to do except play competitive Frisbee or air guitar to the latest Government Mule CD—is fond of toasting the experience by quaffing astonishing quantities of Coors Light.

---

1. What sort of name is Rudyard?

Bavarian White Guy is legendary for guzzling monstrous steins of Pilsner, particularly during October, when the harvest is in the barn and the oompah and *die fräulein* are at their ripened best.

Australian White Guy enjoys beer together with a few shrimp on the barbie, a few Sheilas in their shorts serving them and a good, brisk, limb-snapping game of Aussie rules football on the plasma telly, mate.

Canadian White Guy prepares for the beer season at the cottage by consuming copious amounts at the pub during the spring, watching the NHL playoffs, being interrupted on occasion by frantic text messages from the wife and children, trying to determine whether or not he's still alive. He is alive, at least until the Senators get knocked out again and a franchise from the Deep South wins the Cup, which is when Canadian White Guy pulls out the hard stuff and really starts to pound drinks.

American White Guy's favourite beer is thought to be the last one in the parking lot of his home NFL football team, consumed in a single continuous quaff, twenty minutes before kickoff, before any regular season game. The fact that this drink is drunk outdoors, in a northeastern city in December, in sub-zero temperatures, does nothing to diminish the pleasure of knowing some loser inside the stadium just paid $8.50 for the exact same beer.

U.K. White Guy prefers his beer warm and in pints, at the local pub, where he goes to engage in spirited debate about the issues of the day, such as the moral legitimacy of the Iraq War or the price of flights to the Canary Islands, at least until the eighth or ninth one, when he just wants to fight someone, preferably some posh wanker with a famous father in the House of Lords who lives off a trust fund.

Wine has been a favourite mood-altering substance of the white guy for twenty centuries or more. Connoisseurs of the grape include Art Opening White Guy, Foodie White Guy and Napa Valley White Guy, or anyone else who makes the pilgrimage to the Napa Valley, Bordeaux, the medieval hill towns of Tuscany or any of the other wine-producing regions of the world, excluding Long Island, where the Long Island Expressway kind of spoils the romance.

Whiskey is the rich relative to beer, the substance that white guys of substance prefer to consume, particularly single malt whiskey, which is truly the amber nectar. White guys of a certain age, such as my dad, who have made it through adolescence (both theirs and their kids), the work years and the tenth, twentieth, and fortieth wedding anniversaries, now spend their days secretly plotting to hang out with their grandchildren and spoil them rotten and enjoy nothing more than to toast the end of another day (still ticking!) with a glass of some single malt—neat, with maybe a splash of tap water. If they're from Manitoba, where the only things people really care about are the weather and finding deals, this drink is washed down with numerous anecdotes about paying well under retail while narrowly avoiding freezing to death on the walk to Shoppers Drug Mart to pick up your prescriptions.

Single malt whiskey is also well known as a global form of currency that can obtain the bearer entree into some of the most secretive societies the world has to offer. If you doubt me, just show up at the North Korean border with a case of eighteen-year-old Macallan and see how long it takes you to be watching bootlegged Judd Apatow comedies in the palace home theatre with Kim Jong-il.

We are guys. We are white. Here are our (car) keys. Hide them. Please. And pour us one more, would you?

Weed, AKA Marijuana, AKA The Chronic, AKA Pot, AKA Dope, AKA 4:20

Weed is beloved by many white guys—those who prefer a quick hit to a cup of coffee when they wake up in the morning. Unlike alcohol, weed is still illegal pretty much everywhere, although there is not much in the way of social stigma involved for people who smoke it, particularly in Vancouver, where smoking cigarettes is a social crime just a notch below pedophilia, but lighting up a fatty at a concert or in any alleyway off Granville Street is as socially acceptable as wearing Ducati racing gear to a business lunch.

While it doesn't exactly focus your work ethic or steer you into solid nutritional decision-making, marijuana itself is a relatively benign mood-altering substance. Weed Loving White Guy tends to be an easy-going, associative, imaginative, non-narrative driven guy who loves jam bands and has never met a slide guitar solo that couldn't go a few minutes longer.

I did my share of sampling as a teen, but weed never really caught on with me. As a teenager out on Friday nights in Winnipeg, I often found myself cruising the streets of St. James with Chase, my large, dopey buddy who was a kind of human St. Bernard. Chase loved weed, so I smoked it with him in order to be polite—a bad reason to break the law, but that's recreational Canadian drug use for you.

Chase loved muscle cars. I forget what his was—it was red, domestic and two-doored—but the final act of a Friday or Saturday night usually consisted of smoking a bowl or two, listening to *Best of Budgie* and going to the A&W at Polo Park for a Teen Burger and a root beer to talk muscle car trash with a lot of weed-smoking, muscle-car loving Winnipeg white guys I wouldn't normally have been caught dead with.

Chase and I would sit in his red, pinstriped muscle car munching out at two in the morning, with the heavy metal screaming in our ears, gazing, bleary-eyed, out at the traffic driving past us along Portage Avenue, the city's main drag. Beyond Portage lay the vast, concrete empty parking lot of Polo Park Shopping Mall. It was often twenty or thirty below zero.

Quite often, the hood of our car would be up. The hood of every guy's car would be up, at every bay of the A&W, the better for the other guys to check out each other's engine size. They would drift by our car and peek into Chase's engine and ask what he had.

"What you got, a 363?"

"454," Chase would say. They were talking cubic inches.

They would chat like this, out in the freezing, middle-of-the-night chill, while I sat inside, in the passenger seat of the car, vaguely paranoid because of the bowls I had smoked, listening to some heavy metal band I could not bear, wondering if I had been reincarnated as a suburban, Winnipeg-residing, dope-smoking, Judas Priest-listening, 1970s teenager because of some heinous crime I'd committed in an earlier life.

Maybe I hadn't. But there I was, nevertheless. I was always searching for new experiences, and this was definitely that, only less so.

Winnipeg is a tough town. The economy in Winnipeg is as flat as the landscape. These were tough, muscle car kinds of guys—the sort of guys you'd cross the street to avoid. Winnipeg is full of guys like that, the kind who want to fight you just because they're stuck in Winnipeg.

Only once you got into their inner muscle car circle, once you got a glimpse, they weren't very tough guys at all. They were just anxious white guys who didn't really have anything to brag about, except the size of the engine in their car. All the dope and heavy metal and A&W food—which did taste good after a few bowls—was just a cover story for what they really hungered for, which was love.

Twelve Steps to Trouble

The narcotic family that starts happily enough with pot quickly degenerates into a series of powerful, mood-and-behaviour-altering substances that are not benign and can quickly cause their users to deteriorate into socially maladjusted addicts—which, of course, is part of these substances' appeal, particularly among younger white guys who have no deep, dark secrets and are looking for a second act for their memoir.

In the early twenty-first century, two of the most popular harder drugs are OxyContin and crystal meth. The former is a simu-lated heroin used for pain relief, whereas the latter is some sort of extreme stimulant—a cross between amphetamines and mainlining two dozen café américanos—manufactured in the bathtubs of trailer park owners throughout the American Midwest.

Crystal meth is famously favoured by White (Trash) Guy, who is easily identified by his ever-present wife-beater, emaciated frame, long, greasy hair and uneven or absent teeth.[2] Crystal Meth White Guy is paranoid and highly flammable, and should be avoided at all times.

OxyContin is the preferred mood-alterer of people such as Rush Limbaugh, the famed talk-radio personality, who spent a long time calling people who become addicted to mood-altering substances moral reprobates who vote Democrat, before confessing that he was addicted to the stuff, too.

There are also classic mood-altering substances such as heroin and cocaine, both of which are synonymous with the rock and roll and Hollywood lifestyles, although crack cocaine has been making inroads into some unlikely places, such as the oil patch of Fort McMurray, Alberta, where the workers earn too much money and have too little to do, so they get together after the hard work is done for the day to smoke a little crack.

In the more pastoral parts of the planet, such as Wales and the Gulf Islands of British Columbia, not to mention at summer music festivals everywhere, there is still much love for magic mushrooms and acid, both hallucinogens designed to make the user think the world is beautiful and the band to whom they are listening is speaking only to them.

These sorts of substances are best ingested during the summer months in fenced-in fields ringed with port-a-potties. Although horror stories abound of misguided users mistakenly thinking they can fly and hurling themselves off the roofs of buildings, the usual result of taking acid or 'shrooms is lots of bad, overly contorted dancing by W People in their thirties and forties (and these

---

2. Not to be confused with Kid Rock, who just plays White (Trash) Guy on stage.

days, fifties and sixties) who haven't danced for years and want to give their ramrod hamstrings a little workout on the grass next to the stage at the local folk fest. The only real suffering is that experienced by people sitting close by, who aren't on anything, particularly the drug-user's children, if they made the mistake of coming along to see Joe Cocker with dad.

The world's number one mood-altering substance, however, is still coffee. Coffee Drinking White Guy has been immortalized in the form of Dr. Frasier Crane, the ravingly egotistical, over-analytical radio host, and his neurotic therapist brother Niles, who live in Seattle, home of the ubiquitous Starbucks coffee chain, which now has something like 13,000 outlets worldwide.

Coffee Drinking White Guy is everywhere, particularly at work, his preferred habitat. He is animated, happy, alert. He is often seen double-fisting, coffee in one hand and Blackberry in the other, sucking back caffeine and digesting email simultaneously while listening to Jim Rome on the radio.

Coffee Drinking White Guy is apt to be chatty, which is not characteristic of the general species of White Guy, which tends to crowd towards the non-verbal side of the humanity chart. The good news: this species of white male is thought to be generally harmless, although it can be hazardous to meet him for the first time after swapping several dozen emails on some networking/dating/friends website, only to make the jarring discovery that he is only four and a half feet tall and likes to talk. A lot. About himself.

Ten Great Places to Get F'ed Up

10. Bonnaroo, Tennessee. Dude. You bring the mushrooms, I'll bring the Jack and magical things will happen when Amy Winehouse begins to play.

9. Opening Day, your favourite Major League Baseball stadium. Still happens in the afternoon, in the first week of April. Chances are the weather won't be great. You really ought to be at work. Oh, Christ. Why not have another?

8. Grossman's Tavern, Spadina Avenue, Toronto. Saturday afternoon jazz in the loveliest dive bar on the Spadina strip.

7. The Lower East Side. The New York City neighbourhood where all the immigrants settled in the early twentieth century is now hip and full of great bars. The epicentre is Max Fish, on Ludlow Street.

6. The Marais, Paris. Okay, you need to take out a mortgage to be able to afford Paris. For another thing, there are no A&Ws to hang out in at 2 AM checking out the engines of French White Guy's Citroen Deux Chevaux. And besides, some angry immigrant set the car on fire last week.

5. Burning Man. Nothing like a Nevada desert and a $300 cover charge and no showers for ten days to make a guy want to get naked and express himself.

4. Thursday nights. Way more fun than Friday and Saturday nights, when the pressure is on to have an incredible time.

3. Your ex-girlfriend's wedding. Her old man is paying for you to drink a bottle of wine, three or four beers and a dozen mixed drinks, then vomit in the handicapped stall of the country club/ tenth-century French chateau/historical landmark hotel/church basement. It's the worst night of your life. Have at it.

2. Vegas, baby, Vegas. I'll say this about the (garish, loud, tacky, cheesy, vulgar, hot, crowded, expensive) Strip: it's definitely walking-friendly. And the air conditioning really rocks once you've sweated through the back of your shirt.

1. JazzFest, New Orleans. Don't opt for the cliché that is Bourbon Street. The truly discerning N'awlins drunk hangs on Frenchman Street, just north of the French Quarter.

Chapter Summary

One of the white guy's favourite leisure time activities is to ingest a few substances and alter his mood. While the intentions behind these actions are frequently a good time, the results are often verbal abuse, ill-advised gunplay and horrific dancing.

HABITAT

—— *or* ——

HOME AND HEARTH

• • •

WHITE GUY HAS always believed in home ownership. He used to live downtown, but then, in the 1920s, '30s and '40s, when Non-White Guy moved in next door because he'd found a job in the Ford motor works, White Guy began to look longingly towards the outskirts. And so were born The Suburbs, hatched from a potent brew of fear, social anxiety and a desperate desire to live in homes with one big back yard, two SUVs, a three-car garage, four flat screen TVs, five big bedrooms, six personal computers, seven walk-in closets, eight used coffeemakers, nine abandoned Walkmans, ten misplaced hockey pucks, eleven kinds of breakfast cereal, twelve styles of jogging shoe—and a gun collection, in case of surprise visitors.

Meet Cul-de-Sac White Guy (CdeSWG): he lives in a world that's hard to find, harder to get out of, on streets often named after poets or nature, both of which have been obliterated in order to build another forty thousand homes that look exactly like the one he lives in.

Twenty-five years ago, however, things were clearer. There was CdesWG, there was Downtown Non-White Guy, and never the twain should meet. Now things are different. Sort of. For one thing, CdesWG Guy's neighbour is just as likely to be Cul-de-Sac Non-White Guy, who is just as interested in security systems and the whereabouts of the closest Home Depot, and is absolutely terrified of Downtown Non-White Guy, too.

He's not so crazy about Downtown Artsy White Guy either, particularly when he shows up Sunday night and parks his oil-dripping, twenty-year-old Volvo beater on the cul-de-sac in order to sponge a meal off the in-laws and maybe snag some gently used jogging shoes off little brother, who works in retail.

Many of these neighborhoods now are governed by homeowners associations who restrict the colours they can paint their homes, on the presumption that nothing beats beige. In Calgary, they got the great idea to give all the streets in a given neighborhood the exact same name. Hence, you have Edgewood Drive, Edgewood Crescent, Edgewood Close, Edgewood Avenue, etc., etc. Every one is lined with large, cookie-cutter, beige homes.

Last year, Mel, our then three-year-old son Gus and I were driving to visit my brother Keith in his suburban neighborhood. Gus was excited because Uncle Keith has an impressive collection of toys, including a fine Superman action figure, so he was pumped up to get there.

Looking out the window from the vantage point of his kid's car seat, Gus summed up the suburbs better than Jane Jacobs ever could have. "Is that Uncle Keith's house?" he asked. We kept driving, past one identical house after another. "Is that Uncle Keith's house, is that Uncle Keith's house, is that Uncle Keith's house, is that Uncle Keith's house, is that Uncle Keith's house?"

Hey—it's a great neighbourhood to raise kids in.

Notes from the Summer of Lawn

While CdeSWG tends to live in a house that looks exactly like the house next door, which looks exactly like the house next door, which looks exactly like the house next door, which looks ex—

Did the keyboard develop a stutter?

—there are a few ways CdeSWG expresses his suburban individuality.

Take the lawn.

Lawn and white guys have been as inextricably connected as Lennon and McCartney, Hall and Oates, and Hillary and Bill, ever since the first suburb was built, in Levittown, Long Island, right after World War II. To live in the suburbs and be a guy is to be defined by your lawn. I know that's the way it was at my house.

My dad was a lawn perfectionist. He was an army dentist. Digest that one for a moment. Not only was he the *Prince of Tides*, he was also that Dr. Mengele-esque character Sir Laurence Olivier played in *Marathon Man*—all in the same person! My dad was the most reliable person alive, but he was also a little obsessive about the details, which is good if you're a dentist, but can get weird out in the rest of life.

When I was eleven, we moved from a rental in the rough and tumble Winnipeg North End to a cul-de-sac named Pinewood Drive in the more prosperous suburb of St. James. Across the street from our home on Pinewood Drive was a German university professor named Klaus Wrogeman and his wife Dorit, who had two sons who loved botany.[1] Next door on the left was Abe Schmidt, a contractor with two sons named Colin and Dewey. On the other side of us were the LePages, who owned a steakhouse called The Paddock. They were a family of dandies, people who knew about wine, who vacationed every winter in Florida. Mr. LePage had a vaguely Euro air about him, too—something not quite Western

---

1. I'm not implying having sons who love botany is a bad thing. Maybe I am.

Canadian—but even more critical, didn't give a crap about his lawn—didn't weed it, forgot to water it, but mostly, gave the impression that he had more important things to be concerned about than the lawn.

Which drove Dad crazy.

Dad would ship in fertilizer and spread it over the lawn in the spring. He would weed it. Since I was the oldest kid, it was my job to mow the lawn. I would rebel against the rigid, conservative method by mowing the lawn in expressionistic swirls, bringing a whiff of the Cedar Tavern and Jackson Pollock to the front of our home on Pinewood Drive. This didn't go over too well with Dad. ("If you're going to cut lawn like that, go cut LePage's lawn.")

Now, I am thrilled to report, I have come across a new book called *American Green: The Obsessive Quest for the Perfect Lawn* by Ted Steinberg, an environmental historian at Case Western Reserve University in Cleveland. It's hard to believe a guy could write a whole book about lawn care, but Professor Steinberg did. In the book he describes the pursuit of lawn perfection as a kind of obsessive-compulsive behaviour. Like Attention Deficit Disorder, they didn't have a name for this when I was sixteen—or maybe they did.

It was "Dad."

Before I finished writing this book, Mel, Gus and I moved from an apartment in Santa Monica to a (rented) house in Calgary, with a lawn. It was my first lawn in twenty-five years. A rental lawn, granted, but isn't there just something about lawn and white guys that goes together like chips and salsa?

The more I live here, the more I care about the damn lawn.

I cut it. I pull the weeds from it. I rake it. When it's raining, I gaze out the window and admire it. If I were W.H. Auden and living in the English countryside instead of an entertainment reporter living in downtown Calgary, I'd write a poem about it.

This section will have to do.

Mel, on the other hand, has—how shall I put it?—a very indifferent relationship with the lawn. The lawn barely registers with her. I can tell lawn means way more to me than it does to her, just like she is way more attuned to clothes than I am.

Our first Summer of Lawn was a beautiful summer, but we spent hardly a moment hanging out in the back yard. We had been living in big cities for so long, we didn't know how to *have* a back yard. The back yard just sat there the whole summer, lovely and ignored, gazing back at us, as we sat in the kitchen trying to figure out where the wall that blocked our view went.

When I told Melanee about the book about white guys' obsessive compulsive disorder and lawn, she said it was a reflection of the W Person's anxiety about needing to control nature, which is why we have always excelled at hedge-cutting, tree-pruning, baseball-park construction and golf-course design.

She may have a point there.

Summer Habitat: Cottage Country

In those regions of the world blessed with abundant lakes and verdant trees sprouting between the achingly beautiful mountains, there lies a hidden world filled with mosquitoes, outhouses, decks, pitchers of gin, the wafting scent of grilled meat and, occasionally, the piercing cry of Waterskiing White Guy meeting shallow rock in deep lake.

Cottage country.

In the earliest days of cottage country, the cottage wasn't much. It was little more than an ice-fishing shack thrown up on solid (frozen?) ground. That was the way Summer Home White Guy liked things at his summer home: hard. No indoor plumbing. Kerosene lamps, the better to get the kids to fall asleep by sundown, and cold lakes to jump into when the midday sun grew hot.

Of course, as the years have gone by, cottage country has evolved into its own, unofficial version of the gated community.

After all, wasn't the point of cottage country to get away from it all? What do you think "it all" was?

What Cottage Country White Guy never really counted on, is that not everyone is very into the idea of cottage country.

For one thing, cottages cost a lot these days. Those ice-fishing shacks have been replaced by little mini-Taj Mahals with A-frame windows, the better to admire sunset over a pitcher of drink without getting chewed alive by the skitters.

For another thing, a lot of non-white guys don't see the point of spending tens of hundreds of thousands of dollars in order to do it yourself. The non-white guy might have tens of thousands of dollars to spend in his leisure time, and guess what? He doesn't want to catch fish and then fillet them. He doesn't want to lather on sunscreen and industrial strength bug spray so he can pick blueberries under a noonday August sun. He doesn't want to chop kindling so he can build himself a bonfire.

Non-white guys would just as easily hit Vegas, London, the casinos at Macao or some resort on Phuket, where you get four-star service for about the same money. It turns out that cottage country, like a lot of W ideas, is a W thing.

Although I am a white guy, I pretty much missed cottage country, even though I grew up in Winnipeg, the land of 100,000 lakes, where cottage country is affordable for almost anyone.

We couldn't afford one—at least not until I was eighteen. We were slow to break into property ownership.

We eventually moved from our hard scrabble North End rental to a middle-class suburb called St. James, which was filled with cottage-country people. Every summer they would disappear for weeks or months to places with seductive-sounding names like Victoria Beach, Falcon Lake, West Hawk or Lake of the Woods. I never really knew what went on at cottage country, although whenever those guys talked about it, I acted like I did.

A couple of times, they invited me to their cottages and I went.

I didn't much like it in cottage country. I wasn't into water sports. Nature makes me anxious. I missed cities, even Winnipeg. I missed watching sports on TV.

Okay. Full disclosure: I had to stay home and re-mow the damn *lawn*.

We're Coming to Ten Neighbourhoods Near You,[2]
or Gentrification Is Just Another Way of Saying, Woke Up This Morning and Guess What? The New Neighbours are W People.

1. Harlem. It's got brownstones, Bubba, Central Park and its dirty little secret—a Fairway Grocery Store, at 137th and Riverside. *Perfect.*

2. South Central L.A. Soon it will be Crips, Bloods and White Guys Just Back From Home Depot.

3   The Banlieu, Paris. That's a pretty way of saying the suburbs that burned in the autumn of '05.

4. Baghdad. What they need to do is build golf courses and condos, and the retirees will follow. Baghdad needs retirees. A lot of retirees.

5. Buffalo, New York. Looking a lot like the last place in New York State to gentrify. Anyone want a deal on an NFL team?

6. Union City, New Jersey. The secret enclave that's a mere $2 shuttle bus and ten minutes from Manhattan. Makes Brooklyn real estate look like the Upper East Side.

7. Queen Charlotte Islands, B.C. Lots of waterfront property here. Global warming could be the best thing to ever happen to this rainforest.

8. Iran. No more bearded presidents, *fatwas* and nuclear energy. If Dubai can be the Vegas of the Middle East, why can't Tehran be Palm Springs?

---

2. Starbucks, The Gap, Whole Foods and a Whole Lotta W People.

9. Winnipeg. Hey Gretzky! We built an arena! Give back the Jets, and downtown is sure to follow.

10. Mexico. Housing prices in Southern California got you down? Has North America priced itself out of reach? I have four words: Mexican. Colonial. Fixer-Upper.

Chapter Summary

When it comes to home, the White Guy likes bigger, newer and farther from the threats his life is filled with. It's a great place to raise kids.

SPIRITUAL BELIEFS

—— *or* ——

THE THINGS THAT MATTER MOST

• • •

God, or Whatever

WITH THE NOTABLE exceptions of Alberta and its sister region, the United States, God is dead for most white guys around the world. Since Dublin real estate boomed, even the Irish have given up on God, and who would have thought that would happen? In lieu of God, the White Guy has embraced a number of different spiritual beliefs, including work, technology, money, celebrity and economic growth; more on those below. But first, one of the last true remaining white guy gods: Nothing, as worshipped by Secular Humanist White Guy (SHWG, pronounced "Seinfeld").

SHWG believes in himself, in other people, and in reasonableness prevailing in the end. SHWG invariably comes out on the side of science, rather than faith. While this conjures up images of loser guys in lab coats standing in a room quoting old episodes of *Frasier* to one another rather than joining in rousing, uplifting spirituals,

I have to admit that one look at the news from the Middle East, where God is still very much alive, makes secular humanism look awfully good.

It all sounds terribly, terribly reasonable—but that's the rub, isn't it?

Reasonableness is a spiritual belief, the same way having no racial experience is a racial experience. If you start by assuming that people are calm and reasonable, you're going to run into road-blocks the moment you start exporting your cultural values and telling people to be reasonable and do exactly what you tell them to. Sometimes they don't react in an entirely reasonable fashion.

I know, because it happens at my house every day.

From the way Mel drops God into every other monologue she delivers around our house, you would think she had the guy on speed dial. What exactly constitutes her spiritual side is subject to a certain amount of fluctuation—some days it's Buddha, other days it's old (Catholic) school God—but we did live for nine years in California, where spiritual beliefs are sort of like Asian fusion cooking: you take a bit from here (inner serenity), a bit from there (miracles do happen) and stir it all into a thing you call your spiri-tual beliefs (if I believe I will be cast in a hit series on HBO, it will happen).

My first reaction to having God become a part of the conversa-tion around our house was to become uncomfortable, probably for no other reason than if there is one, I figured all the white guys in the world were in deep trouble.

Who declared God dead? I'm not sure, but if I had to guess, I'd say it was early twentieth century, World War I–ravaged intellectual Euro White Guy living in his freezing cold apartment in downtown Paris, unable to scratch together the *centimes* for a glass of *cabernet* at the bistro downstairs, so there you go: millions are dead in the trenches and what good did that do? I'm still cold, sober and single.

God must therefore be dead! *Le mort!*

Not that God didn't have a good run. For a few thousand years, a lot of white guys in some of the most powerful corner offices on the planet have pretty much had God on the board of executives, signing off on every corporate decision, whether it's to close the plant and un-employ thousands, un-elect the local government or pre-emptively invade some backwards country for their own benefit. God has always been the great moral equalizer, and trust me, the white guy throughout history knew about staking out the moral high ground long ago and far away (see chapter 10: The White Guy in Human History).

Melanee, when she isn't talking about God, is often buried in a self-help book, which is basically the contemporary, secular substitute for The Good Book. She loves self-help books. I don't believe I have ever read one, although to be fair, I have subscribed to *Sports Illustrated* for close to thirty years now, and *Sports Illustrated*, with its ongoing narrative of American Athlete Guy overcoming the odds to win at whatever he does, is pretty much a self-help book, in addition to having an impressive swimsuit issue every February.

Bottom line: God is dead! So let's be reasonable, okay?

Ten White Guy Gods

10. Jesus Christ. Still popular among Mel Gibson fans, in regions of the Southeastern United States, Orange County and rural Alberta.
9. Steve Jobs. Inventor of Apple Computers, Pixar, the iPod, the iPhone and wearing jeans and sneakers to work. We love him!
8. The Blackberry. For those who worship at the altar of never being out of touch.
7. Steven Spielberg. The guy's Jewish, he's got a beard, he grew up in the (Arizona) desert. He got crucified for *1941*, but resurrected himself quite nicely with thirty years of mega-hits.
6. Michael Jordan. Technically not a white guy, but a legend among white guys for his athleticism, competitive drive and endearingly mediocre golf game. Ditto (though with a much better golf game)

Tiger Woods. A prophet from tee to green and a serene, dead-perfect Buddha from twenty feet and in.

5. The Dalai Lama. Quite the guru for Non-Violent, Yoga-Practicing, Vegetarian White Guy. What's a Lama?

4. Bill Clinton. Democrat icon who ran the country into a surplus and didn't start any wars.[1]

3. Brett Favre. Beloved Packers quarterback in the most popular white guy sport of them all.

2. Dale Earnhardt, Sr. NASCAR legend who died tragically at Daytona, a fact that only elevates him in everyone's mind.

1. Bruce Springsteen. Working-class poet with a guitar and a plaid shirt. Icon of a generation of white guys, who regularly pray at the altar of Bruce.

Alternative White Guy Gods No. 1: Work

The white guy everywhere is known for his prodigious appetite for employment, although less so in certain hamlets of Atlantic Canada between October and April every year. This in itself is not unique to guys who are white; guys everywhere like to work. Or at least guys like to be employed. Where white guys take it one step further is that we define ourselves by our work.

What distinguishes the White Guy—at least to this point in human history—is that he has managed to hog almost all of the good jobs, aside from most starting fives in the NBA, the mayor of L.A. and Secretary of State, at least since the fall of the Muslim Caliphate early in the eighth century. Anywhere there's a hint of a respectable job, and frequently a lot of unrespectable ones, there's excellent odds there will be some white guy who knows someone who knows someone in Human Resources.

The White Guy turned white by habituating the colder corners of the world, and as one white guy who habituated Winnipeg—

---

1. Okay, he bombed Kosovo. And Iraq. Several times. And that alleged arms factory in the Sudan that turned out to be a pharmaceutical plant. But no big wars.

the coldest city in the world with a population over 100,000—
the rule of thumb when it's –37°F outside with a 30 mph north-
northwesterly wind blowing at you is, *keep moving.*

Human history takes a long time to unfold, and while the first
three thousand years or so could be regarded as a success story
for the White Guy with regards to work, times are getting tough.
Rapid technological change—along with the feminist revolution,
the rise of the global economy and general weariness—have sig-
nificantly eroded the White Guy's ability to hog all the worthwhile
jobs everywhere, particularly the sidekick's anchor role on the evening newscast.

Is work a spiritual belief? It always was in our house growing up,
where you could get out of any obligation by claiming a need to
work. Work was the number one priority, and I suspect it still is in a
lot of White Guy houses.

That said, the nature of work is changing with the world, creating new subsections of white guys who work part time, or
occasionally, or not at all. The *New York Times* recently ran an article about middle-aged white guys dropping out of the workforce
because they couldn't locate jobs they felt matched their earlier
work, and they didn't have a compelling enough reason to take
jobs that paid less. The *Los Angeles Times'* Molly Selvin wrote an
article about the increasing trend of wives earning more than their
husbands, and how the husbands are okay with that. According to
Stephanie Coontz, a historian at Evergreen State University who
has written books on marriage and gender roles, "Men are saying,
'I don't mind being married to a woman who earns more than I,'
and women are giving up the notion that they have to find a man
who can support them."

There are also lots of educated, young white guys in their twenties who find it difficult to break into the workplace and question
the workplace itself.

Why work? What is it all for? Why give forty years of your
life to a company who employs supervisors who get promoted by

identifying people they can fire? If companies are going to be indifferent to their employees, why should employees buy into the company line? These are just some of the questions that Twenty-something White Guy might find himself asking as he idles away another afternoon in the Starbucks adjoining the Barnes and Noble magazine rack.

The thing of it is, all of these are valid, thoughtful questions. They are kind of like the questions French philosophers used to ask back in the day about the existence of God, which were a great way to pick up women at French philosophy parties—except the ones where you got struck, purely at random, by lightning.[2]

Melanee doesn't share my belief in the spiritual power of work, however. She's not a member of the White Guy Church of 9 to 5. In addition to being a non-white, non-guy, she's an actor. Actors aren't quite painters, who will eat paint before getting a job, but they're the next best thing.

Actors not only spend their lives trying to hit the lotto; they are the lotto. Every morning, they wake up and think, maybe *today* will be my day. They take jobs between real (acting) jobs in order to survive. They have no reference for life other than the momentary, the transitional, the day-to-day life that most people never led, not even as college students. Actors, to tell you the truth, aren't really people at all; they just play people. When they're not working, they're absolute disasters, a mess of anxiety, neediness and occasional megalomania interrupted from time to time by sweeping, epic bouts of self-doubt. Couple this with the fact that they tend to be cuter than the general population, and you have a real recipe for disaster.

---

2. See Audrey Hepburn and Fred Astaire in *Funny Face*, the movie that *The Devil Wears Prada* wanted to be. Audrey is a cute West Village bohemian who dreams of going to France to meet her idol, a French philosopher who preaches "empathicalism."

All of which is what led me to understand that not everyone worships at the Temple of Work. Work can be just as much of a false idol as any other god out there.

That said, it was a nice run that white guys were on. It's tough to complain. It might be a hard couple of centuries coming up, but we'll always have our memories. Was it a three-thousand-year-long bubble? Ask Alan Greenspan. But hurry—he's eighty.

Ten Favourite White Guy Jobs

10. President of the United States Guy. Upside: Exceptionally long hours, but high quality of international swag when visiting other heads of state. Downside: Occasional wars, scandals and economic downturns to contend with, not to mention the aggravation when your man in Pakistan declares martial law and suspends the constitution.

9. Late Night Talk Show Host Guy. Downside: no one is funny ninety minutes a night, five days a week. Upside: it pays about $14 million a year, not bad for a geeky, ex-weatherman from Indiana with a chipped tooth, or a motorcycle-driving standup with a lantern jaw, or a six-eleven white guy with Jimmy Neutron hair, or a frustrated sports columnist, or stream-of-consciousness Scottish guy trying desperately to locate sun screen that is 75 SV.

8. CEO Guy. Upside: private plane, $25 million a year in stock options, lots of golf. Downside: keeping those quarterly reports on the upswing at all costs, which will likely involve: cutting the pay of the sweatshop employees, burning a hole in the ozone, overthrowing the people's elected government—they don't know what's good for them—and most of all, scalping hydro electricity to California at rates that would make the Ticketmaster blush.

7. AM Drive-Time Talk Radio Guy. Upside: talking for a living. Being the first one up in the city every morning. Light traffic on the drive to work. Downside: those 3:30 AM wake up calls put a real dent in your nightlife, reading those sponsor plugs sucks big-time and

what—exactly—is the difference between what you
do and that chipped-tooth ex-Indiana weatherman who bags
$14 million a year to schmooze with Paul Shaffer every night
on national TV?

6. Middle East Foreign Correspondent Guy. Upside: you don't have
   to be stuck in the office, pretending to be working. Downside:
   beheading.
5. Golf Pro Guy. Upside: no cubicle, a nice markup on the pro
   shop merchandise, the yearly junkets to Hilton Head. A lot of
   bored, wealthy wives. Downside: being so close to being a touring
   pro—and yet so far.
4. Off Broadway, Not-for-Profit, Artistic Director Guy. Upside: all
   those pretty boys looking for a part! Downside: patrons with a play
   in their drawer that they wrote twelve years ago, which they are
   absolutely convinced will really resonate in today's political climate.
3. Office Manager Guy. Upside: a lot of meetings, where you get first
   crack at the fresh pastries. Monitoring everyone's email. Downside:
   telling 80 percent of the staff their jobs just got outsourced to a call
   centre in Bangalore, and being expected to feel their pain.
2. Movie Director Guy. Upside: The travel, the stories you get to tell,
   the girls! Downside: getting the call Friday night at 8:15 PM telling you that your $150 million Middle Ages epic is on track to
   gross $11 million. Worldwide.
1. Wealth Management Guy. Upside: flying to Turks and Caicos
   on clients' dime to discuss portfolio. Hearty year-end bonuses.
   Expensing five-figure club memberships. Downside: earning low
   seven figures every year and still being the poorest guy in the
   foursome. Has anyone heard of any good deals on a used Learjet?

Alternative White Guy Gods No. 2:
Technology, or Can I Get a Gigabyte of That?
Technology, needless to say, has improved our lives considerably
since the eleventh century, when everyone's teeth were disgusting, the roads turned to impassable mud whenever it drizzled and

no one ever ate fresh vegetables, or any vegetables for that matter except what was growing in the backyard. Nowadays, we purify, organicize,[3] digitize, download and upload our entire lives. We also have fluoride in our tap water, a prescription for every ailment and an impressive array of long-distance calling plans that stretch to every corner of the planet.

Yes, the technology we have is astonishing, and it has invaded every single aspect of our lives. There is a certain sort of white guy who has made it his life's mission to own nothing but the best, most state-of-the-art technology that exists, even if by doing so he turns himself into a round-the-clock workaholic who's so permanently wired he can't escape from the world for five minutes without sinking into an irretrievable morass of sensory deprivation.[4]

People like my brother. Ever since we were kids, my brother has been in love with technology. When he was about eleven, the song "Convoy" was a hit, which ignited the CB radio craze. He was determined to own a CB radio. We lived in the Winnipeg suburbs, so what he planned to do with his CB radio was beyond me. I don't think he longed to chat with lonely long-distance truckers, although it could be something he's been keeping from me all these years. He just thought owning a Citizen's Band radio would be cool.

The only problem was, my mom wouldn't let him buy one.

He wasn't very good with money, because technology inhales money. Also—let's face it—he was eleven. Unless you're Macaulay Culkin or an Olsen twin, there's just not a lot of money out there for eleven-year-olds to earn. The only way he was going to be able to afford a CB radio was if my dad lent him the money, and my dad wasn't exactly loose with the money except—

There were two things my dad responded to with almost Pavlovian certainty: 1. He was a techno-junkie too, and 2. Fear.

---

3. Is that a word?
4. If no one can get a hold of me, do I exist?

Mom continued to say no to a CB radio. Dad sat on the fence. My brother continued to lobby.

One day, I came home from school and discovered him in his room, assembling a new metal detector.

Excuse me?

Metal detectors were something he'd never had the slightest interest in. Until, in all likelihood, he found himself in the park, with no money, wondering how he was ever going to be able to continue to finance his technology habit—and has there ever been a habit more universally applauded by White Guy World than to the use of technology?—when he stumbled upon some nut job waving a metal detector through the grass, wearing those ridiculous headphones in order to hear the beeps when he stumbled across some dirty, bent dime, and my loser brother thought, *aha!*

He used it maybe one time, at which point it disappeared into the technology graveyard otherwise known as the back of his closet.

Then, what seems like weeks later, I come home and discover him fiddling the knobs on not just one, but *two* CB radios.

"Where'd you get those?" I ask. His bedroom, jammed with a stereo, metal detector, various menacing-looking locks and two new CB radios looks a bit like the radio room of a submarine.

"A guy sold me them both for forty bucks," he says. "It's a great deal. They're worth over a hundred. I'll just sell the second one, and make enough to pay for the first one."

Then, it's winter, 1978, and we're driving across northern Michigan, home from Christmas in Toronto, when we run into a raging blizzard. It's ridiculous to try to drive through, but my dad—like every dad—tries, until we are forced to pull off the highway, miles out of the last town, miles from the next town. It's 7 PM on New Year's Eve.

My brother pulls out the CB radio and turns it on. It turns out a trucker going the other way is right on the other side of the trees, and he rescues the five of us and drives into the police station in

Gaylord, where the sheriff on duty takes us to his house and lets us sleep over.

So he was right and I was wrong. I never said I was right! I said Techno White Guy worships at the altar of technology—sometimes with good reason! Maybe God is good enough when you come from some place warm, but blizzard people require radios that work.

Where Were We Again?

Techno white guy is also on prominent display during times of war or, even more prominently, during the lead-up to war. This is when Techno White Guy—frequently ex–Four Star General White Guy under retainer from some billion-dollar weapons manufacturer—announces the end of war as we know it, thanks to some dazzling new device that promises to remove the messiness from the messy business of fighting wars and defeating evil. The smart bomb, nuclear bomb, submarine, fighter jet, Uzi, drone, you name it—at one time or another throughout history, they've been the technology of the moment, and the human cost of fighting wars seemed about to dwindle down to almost none.

The problem with planning wars based on technology is that no one plans for wars to get messy. No one stands in Congress before a vote and goes, "I anticipate that the war we are contemplating will go a hell of a lot worse than we think, because there's never been a war that didn't."

It doesn't matter, though. Give it a few years, and there will be a new group of white guys and a newer, more accurate bomb or killing device, a new global villain, a new Congress and—dare we even mention it?—a new Bush.

Ten Techno Misses

10. The v8 engine. Carbon monoxide? Who gives a damn about carbon monoxide? This is America, brother! We like powerful automobiles.

9. The smart bomb. A bigger oxymoron than "compassionate conservative."

8. The Betamax. Sorry about that, Betamax Inventor Guy, wherever you are.

7. NORAD. It's so cool that we have this bunker in Colorado somewhere where someone is always watching to ensure American airspace never comes under attack. Those tens of billions are what saved us on 9/11.

6. The LCD watch. The kind where you can't see the numbers unless you're in a dark room. Nice idea, vampires.

5. The nuclear bomb. These things were fine when only white guys had them, but now Pakistan and India and South Africa and North Korea have joined the club, not to mention Israel, and suddenly they seem, uh, dangerous.

4. The domestic Humvee. My skin cancer thanks you, auto industry.

3. The electric toothbrush. Battery-industry propaganda.

2. The fat cell phone. The guy who invented this got hired by the Pentagon and talked Rumsfeld into the lean, mean fighting machine mini-army.

1. The eight-track tape. Vinyl? Vinyl? We don't need no stinkin' vinyl! Eight-track!

Alternative White Guy Gods No. 3: Money, or Brother, Can You Spare $4.5 Billion?

Money has no Bible, although one might be tempted to point to any issue of *Vanity Fair*. Money has no Ten Commandments, although "Diversify your portfolio," "Don't spend the principle," "Own, don't rent" and "Location, location, location" might just qualify as a kind of Four Commandments. They aren't haiku or love poems, though, are they? You're not gonna hear some indie band singing their latest single, "Location, Location, Location."

Money has no spiritual leaders, although it does have Warren Buffett, who is close. And Jim Cramer, if you want a screamer.

Money doesn't have any churches, but it does have the mega-malls of Edmonton and Minneapolis, and how many religions would kill to have that sort of parking access to their spiritual temples?

Money doesn't have any sins, although if you miss a payment on your credit card, they have the right to jack your ARP up to about 50 per cent. There are adjustable mortgages coming due left and right, and guess which direction every single mortgage in the world adjusts towards? If you guessed "down," you clearly worship at some temple no self-respecting banker would ever enter.

Ten Ways I've Made Money Along the Way

10. Dancing robot in Rob Zombie video of "Feels So Numb," 2001. Shot in Sylmar, California soundstage. I dressed like C3PO. Danced like a short, white, stiff-limbed James Brown. YouTube it and watch for it, around 3:10 in. I get 1 second. $200

9. Art mover, 1992. Together with my television producer pal Angus Fraser, we drove from New York City to Dallas to Detroit to Cincinnati and back to New York without stopping. All hungover. Barely lived. Learned to use air brakes in the parking lot of the first truck stop we pulled into in northern Virginia. $350.

8. Art gallery dishwasher, Winnipeg Art Gallery, 1985-86. Wrote three drafts of anguished, unpublishable coming-of-age-in-Winnipeg novel by day, washed dishes by night. In retrospect, I should've written a novel about washing dishes in an art gallery. $7.50 per hour.

7. Weekend brunch waiter. Royal Canadian Pancake House, New York City, early 1990s. World's biggest pancakes. Wrote quirky one-act comedies during week, and one-man show called *The White Guy*. $250 per day.

6. Tree planter, Northern Alberta, 1985. They take you deep into the woods, you live in a tent, work fifteen hours a day and the nearest (outdoor) shower, which you get to visit once a week, is six

miles through the woods. Great exercise, though. And what vistas! $48 per day.

5. Star magazine, apprentice gossip reporter, 2002. Went big-game (celebrity) hunting in places like Brentwood and Beverly Hills. Came home empty handed. Fired after three weeks. $1,000 per week.

4. Ghostwriter, screenplay, 2003. Rewrote independent film script for Internet gambling impresario together with Taylor Nichols, star of *Metropolitan* and *Barcelona*. $5,200.

3a. TV pilot writer (CBC), 1988. Wrote original comedy for Canadian television. No go. $3,200.

3b. TV pilot writer (Warner Brothers/Quincy Jones). Wrote original comedy pilot, *The White Guy*, for Telepictures—the same prestige outfit that produces (mega-hit) celeb-slasher show TMZ. No go. $35,000.

2. Internet comedy writer, Comedyworld.com, 2000. Wrote for an Internet comedy radio website with no listeners. Soon thereafter, the website went out of business, having blown $35 million in startup cash in ten months. $1,200 per week.

1. Sold bone marrow, circa 1984. They stick a big, fat needle in your hip and suck out your marrow. Don't try this at home. Probably the worst way a person can earn a hundred bucks (Canadian). $100.

Alternative White Guy Gods No. 4: Celebrity, or Do You Know Who I Am?

Kings and queens were the first white guy celebrities, driving through the village with their entourages, sending personal assistants to pick up the taxes, sleeping with inappropriate commoners, and just generally wreaking havoc, depending on the moon that month. Not to mention deciding to invade England from time to time.

Alas, the decline of monarchies has not led to the decline of famous individuals who act just like kings and queens; quite the contrary. Now, everyone thinks they can do it!

Thanks to evolving technology, such as movies, television, the Internet and the cell phone, the opportunity to be a celebrity has multiplied by ten thousand, giving almost everyone a chance to have an entourage, a personal assistant, a temper tantrum or an affair with the inappropriate person—although you might run into resistance trying to collect taxes from the next door neighbours, or even worse: a nine-millimetre Glock pistol.

At the same time, evolving technology has created ever-larger villages where people do more and more specialized labour that no one really understands. People move frequently, losing touch with family and friends. The world has become connected even as people feel more anonymous than ever.

It's a perfect storm that has created I Wanna Be Famous White Guy (IWBFWG).

IWBFWG is less about money than he is about validation—the validation of a lot of people you've never met, who've never met you and don't really know anything about you or your life, but if they want to buy into the idea that you're special, why the heck not? A lot of time these days, recognition comes at the expense of money, not because of it.

Now, like the entry requirements to the EU, the standards for becoming famous have simply plummeted. Anyone can be famous: a crocodile hunter wearing khakis. A home renovator with perky boobs and a sensible bob. A tattoo artist. A bad ballad singer with a very moving personal backstory. A twenty-two-year-old heroin-addicted, AIDS-infected, male-prostitute-turned-novelist who turns out to be a forty-four-year-old married woman. A first-round draft pick. A seventeen-year-old golfer with an entourage of eleven who turns pro before finishing high school and simply washes out. A guy who drinks Diet Coke and eats Mentos, then posts the results on YouTube.

Working at the Royal Canadian Pancake House in New York in the early 1990s, I had an (admittedly light) brush with worldwide celebrity. One Martin Luther King Day, a CNN crew showed up at my work looking for a holiday story and shot a segment on our gigantic-sized food. Because our restaurant was staffed primarily with illegal immigrants, no one wanted to go on-camera to speak to the reporter.

I was an illegal immigrant too, but at least I was white and a guy, so I somehow got elected to provide the play-by-play as the CNN cameraman panned across our loaf-sized mixed-berry French toast and our hubcap-sized pancakes.

I gave a little show, CNN taped it all, off they went, and I went back to serving pancakes. I didn't watch CNN, never saw the segment, never even thought about it again.

Until about six months later. I'm out with Eric, my Princeton pal who is married to Anne, my old classmate from the University of British Columbia. Eric is a literary agent at one of the top agencies in the world. He moved to New York when I did. He loves baseball, and so do I. In a perfect world, he would be my agent, my champion, my entree into the rarified air of the New York literary scene.

He's not. He never even asks me about my writing. Every time I see him, he tells me about his dreary road trips to the University of Iowa campus, where he meets young, driven, demographically correct graduate student writers and scoops up the most talented.

Or else he flies off to the Frankfurt Book Fair to sell books to publishers from around the world. That's where he's just back from.

"So I'm sitting in a hotel in Frankfurt," he says, "Watching CNN, and what comes on, but a segment about the Royal Canadian Pancake House. Was that you I saw on CNN?"

All I can think about is that dumb yellow badge I've had pinned to my chest for five frigging years of weekend brunches: THINK SAUSAGE.

"Oh," I say, thinking, of all the lies you tell in New York to make it seem like you're doing better than you're really doing. All the goddamn deceptions, and then the one literary agent I happen to know goes halfway around the world, flips on the TV and—

THINK SAUSAGE.

"That was me," I say.

Thinking, I gotta get out of this town.

"You were good on camera," he says.

"Thanks." You bastard.

Chapter Summary

Work, technology and the pursuit of fame and/or wealth have replaced God for many white guys. This is good for the economy, but bad if you are one of those countries on the receiving end of a smart bomb. It can also sabotage your attempts to find quality time to spend with your child.

EMOTIONAL LIFE

• • •

THERE ARE MANY great unsolved mysteries in life. For example, is there life in outer space? Where do we go when we die? Does God exist? How do they get the caramel into a Caramilk bar? These are all humbling, nay, awe-inspiring imponderables, but none of them resonates quite so strongly as the most imponderable of all imponderables: what does the White Guy really feel?

He's a worker. He's a worrier. He's there to pick you up, five minutes before you really need him. He's the president—of whatever. He's on the board of directors—pick a board, any board. He's the owner, the GM, the producer, the director, the head of the studio, the priest, the pope, the lead guitarist, the general, the Nobel Prize laureate for everything except peace (give or take Al Gore). He's the richest guy in the world, someone so smart he made fifty billion bucks peddling software.[1]

---

1. Though it took a woman willing to marry a forty-year-old-virgin-type billionaire before he figured out it feels good to give back a little, too.

He's also the most remote, inaccessible, bottled-up, in-denial, opaque, cold-blooded, mercenary, dysfunctional guy in town.

He's every white guy you ever tried to love.

(Where did it go? Did I miss the day when they handed out feelings? Why do I cry only when I watch one of those excruciating NBC features they run during the Winter Olympics to get us to care about cross-country skiers who also skeet shoot, while during the great emotional moments of my life—birth, death, mortgage rate hikes—my eyes are dry?)

There are no easy answers in a section that attempts to explain the emotional inner life of the White Guy, because we so frequently appear to be missing that chip in our brain that contains our emotional inner life.

On the downside, this has produced many, many generations of emotionally alienated white guys who wouldn't know their hearts if their hearts leapt out of their chests and offered to play *Doom* against them.

On the upside, it has created quite a windfall for fantasy games creators, sports franchise owners and movie studios with the rights to trilogies, because when you're all alone in this world, there's nothing better than lining up for Part II—for a month.

Question: How did the White Guy get so far removed from feeling his feelings, and what will it take to get them back together?

Answer: I don't want to talk about it.

It may have been boarding school. Rupert Everett, the actor who could have had Hugh Grant's career but didn't because he's too camp for Hollywood, wrote a book instead, *Red Carpets and Other Banana Skins*, about his life. It's pretty fab. The childhood part contains a section about Rupe being sent, like many of British Empire White Guy's children, to boarding school to learn the really crucial details about life, like social hierarchy, how to ridicule the weak, and when it is appropriate for men to speak in silly high voices and wear skirts.

Rupe was doted upon as a child by the women in his family, so boarding school came as quite a jolt to his little boy's system— but it turns out, that was exactly what the British Empire had in mind when they invented boarding school! They wanted to churn out leaders, who may in fact have been asked to lead in many of the non-white parts of the world where Britain's long-ago empire existed. This sort of posting frequently involved heart-rending choices that adversely affected the lives of many of the non-white people whom Boarding School British White Guy was in charge of—such as asking the local police constables to round up the usual suspects whenever there was some of that unpleasant grum-bling about the British and their colonizing ways, grumbling that called for a good beating or the odd hanging. Boarding school was the Empire's way of toughening up young men for the task.

Yes, boarding school was emotionally alienating. Yes, the food sucked. Yes, it promoted cliques that evolved into fraternities and secret societies that evolved into the ruling class that eventually ruled millions of people who couldn't stand them. Yes, this may have resulted in generations of myopic, disengaged, paranoid, inept white guys being sent out into the dark corners of the planet when they really just wanted to be back at the cottage with Mum and Aunty, hanging out at the local cinema watching Julie Andrews films. But the Empire needed them, so off they went. Lie back and think of England, Rupe!

Well, the planet took care of that empire. Meanwhile, Ameri-can White Guy continues to lurch around the planet, looking for love in all the wrong places. Who knew replacing British Empire White Guy would be so easy?

The Number Cruncher

The White Guy has an inescapable affinity for numbers. A lot of white guys prefer numbers to people, which only sounds weird if you haven't grown up in a white guy's world. Here, where I live, numbers count. How much money you have. How much you make. How many wives you've had. How many women you've slept with.

And of course, there's the newest numbers tyranny of them all: friends on Facebook.

One of the major emotional obstacles facing Number Crunching White Guy is that, let's face it, relationships are not very numbers-crunchy. In fact, due to their time-consuming nature, their odd emphasis on depth over data, relationships of any sort are Number Crunching White Guy's worst nightmare.

Let us review:

1. When you are in a relationship, it is generally expected that you confine your sexual activity to one (1) other person.

2. By following Item 1, you may well find yourself in a committed relationship, doing things that people in relationships do, like getting married, rather than things you would do if you weren't, such as travelling to every country, trying to sleep with someone representing every living language, or the fallback: seeing a baseball game in every single stadium in North America.[2]

3. If 1 is followed by 2, the result may be a kid or three, which might satisfy a low-hopes number cruncher, but ultimately, children provide love, spontaneity and community, not statistical satisfaction.

When I was in university, I had a friend named Barry. He was one of those brooding, semi-literary, former hockey players with a knee injury who spent a lot of time resenting the hockey players having the career he wasn't going to have.

But then again, Barry was funny. He watched people closely. He was bright, skeptical, independent of mind. We started a moving business one summer, to supplement our unemployment insurance cheques. Okay, it's not exactly starting YouTube, but there was no Internet then. We were from Winnipeg, the place the

---

2. That would be so cool!

global economy forgot, but forty below and waves of mosquitoes could never get enough of. Winnipeggers were raised to aim low and almost reach our dream.

One day, we're sitting in Barry's living room, enjoying the first beer of the afternoon. It's maybe 3 PM.

"Imagine," I say. "Making a thousand dollars a week." We lived quite comfortably, in the mid-'80s in Winnipeg on around $400 a week. A *thousand* bucks a week? Inconceivable.

"What would you do with it if you made that much?" I ask.

Barry thinks about it for a minute.

"Save up and quit my job," he goes.

That was Barry.

The problem was, Barry couldn't quite separate his emotional life from his number-crunching life. He didn't have any career aspirations, except to avoid one. He dropped out of university. He was sort of artsy, but thought artsy people were too into themselves. So he focused all his self-esteem on two things: avoiding full-time employment and seeing how many women he could get to have sex with him.

Next to his never-ending road trip to nowhere, his dream was the grand slam: four different women in four days. At the time, it seemed like something to aspire to.

Alas, Barry was not an anomaly, or a statistical aberration. He was Number Crunching White Guy doing something that has always been highly socially desirable among all guys.

So if you find yourself at some trendy bar with some really cute guy and for some inexplicable reason the conversation turns to numbers, and he really lights up, find a reason to flee. Trust me. To him, you're not a human being; you're a statistic-in-progress.

Chapter Summary

White Guys are the Vulcans of Starship Earth.

• • • • • • • • • • • • • •

MEL'S DEEP THOUGHT

(*Another in an occasional series of interruptions to the narrative flow*)

No. 2: WHITE GUYS ARE AUTISTIC

• • •

I WILL NEVER forget the first time I watched my favourite white-guy actor, Dustin Hoffman, play the Rainman. It broke my heart to see this middle-aged man so unable to process ordinary human interaction that his inconsequential habits—"Gotta go watch Wapner, gotta go watch Wapner..."—took on an emotional significance of great magnitude. Because of his savantism, he was able to make tons of money, his mathematical abilities eclipsing any brain cells that had to do with processing human emotions. And unlike me, he had found a way to shut himself down from other people's emotional complexities and nuances.

I consider the White Guy to be a triumph of autistic mind processes. I figure that in the cold, wintery, overcrowded vistas of Europe, white guys didn't have time to figure out anybody else's emotional states, much less their own. The sun didn't shine half the year and the continent got populated pretty darn quick. The only thing to do was hunt, build and conquer. For "gotta go watch Wapner, gotta go watch Wapner," read "gotta go hunt some food, elbow the competition, build some shelter from this frigging cold."

It is both touching and humbling to see this imperative compel my White Guy husband forward on every front. I have learned that my sensitive, intuitive ability to gauge other people's emotions and reflect upon my own works well with my Rainman husband's ability to count the gumballs in the gumball machine and soothe himself with his version of Wapner—baseball games and the *New York Times*.

End of Deep Thought.

• • • • • • • • • • • • • •

MATING HABITS

. . .

QUESTION: does the section about the sexual habits of white guys go with the section about mating habits, or are they two different chapters altogether?

ANSWER: We're a mess.

Sex

The white guy enjoys the idea of sex more than he actually gets to enjoy having it.

While the popular culture of the White Guy is an ode, a ballad, maybe even a Kennedy Center Tribute to sex in all its rich and myriad forms, the reality of most white guys' lives leaves almost no time to have any.

Being bombarded on a minute-by-minute basis by sexual imagery, which is everywhere—and I mean *everywhere*—fills most white guys with vague longings they can't quite put into words, but let's be realistic: words are vastly overrated when the alternative is Adriana Lima wearing nearly nothing.

Instead, thanks to the evolution of sexually transmitted diseases, cheap, interactive pornography and the high cost of putting your child through the organized hockey system in Canada, the number of white guys actually having sex has been reduced to a precious few, namely George Clooney, Kris Benson (that pitcher married to a former Penthouse Pet who likes to do it in the mini-van parked outside the stadium) and princes Harry and William who, much to the amazement of their inbred family, appear to be normal, functional white guys who happen to be in line to become the King of the Island Formerly Known as the Epicentre of the British Empire.

Cult of the Relationship

Although maybe this is the wrong way to look at it. Maybe the ways in which technology has become the sexual middleman—networking websites, dating websites, instant messaging, online pornography—maybe these still count as sex, in an emotionally detached, twenty-first century, White Guy kind of way.

The White Guy may be having less actual sex than ever, but that hasn't stopped him from pursuing relationships with just about anyone you can think of.

Theoretically, relationships should be wonderful opportunities to have sex. After all, if nothing else, people in relationships frequently live in the same building. There's no commute. There's not even a cover charge. All you really need to do is to listen to a few of her issues, nod sympathetically and say "I know how you feel" over and over and over and over again until an eerie sort of tranquility fills the room, pour some more $10 Argentinean cabernet sauvignon, put on a little James Blunt and watch the clothes fall all around the room.

Either that, or if you're Seventeen-Year-Old White Guy, you can simply hook up under the nearest stairwell, video it on your cell phone and upload it to your MySpace or Facebook profile so your friends can watch.

Enter something larger, something one might even describe as the Al Qaeda of feelings: the Cult of the Relationship. Twenty-first century people spend so much time reading, writing, talking and thinking about relationships, a lot of people have forgotten to have them. Truth be told, a lot of that writing, talking and thinking is done by non-guys trying to understand how guys think. What they don't seem to understand is that guys don't think about relationships at all for very large chunks of their lives. Guys are thinking about other things, like, for example, what happened to the band Toto? Why is having a prominent chin so crucial to national electoral success? Cancun or Costa Rica? Sometimes, these things come disguised as an interest in the relationship, which is where all the trouble starts.

Somehow, white guys have managed to create a media culture where relationships come well down the totem pole in terms of happiness indicators, well below working in the media, obtaining stupefying wealth, travelling to the farthest corners of the globe, being perceived as personal powerhouses and, best of all, being famous. If, somewhere on your journey, you happen to stumble into a lifelong partner and raise a kid or two, well, good on ya, mate.

All of which is a little bit nuts.

After all, when you stop and step back from your material life—your money, toys, vacation plans, weekend plans, career goals—what is the point to any of it if you do it alone? If you live a successful life that no one participates in except you, is that actually a successful life?

No-Kids White Guy

Even odder than the commitmentophobes are the significant number of married white guys who have no kids at all.

If you consider that out of any group of high school buddies, a few will go off into the world to find themselves and a few will get married and settle into stable lives early in life—the weird, mysterious thing about my Winnipeg high school buddies, who are now in their mid-forties, is that a disproportionate number of them got married, settled into stable lives, and totally didn't have a single kid!

What's up with that?

Maybe nothing at all. Maybe they're the new normal.

In fact, a 2006 Stats Can survey revealed that no-children households now make up the majority of households in Canada, for the first time in history.

If there's a single trend that typifies the white guy of the early twenty-first century, it's not the alienated, cybersexed, solitary white guy; rather, it's the married, employed, home-owning, childless white guy.

This white guy grew up in a family, has siblings, goes to his job, comes home to his wife, and decided early on that he didn't want to have any children—and somehow, got her to agree not to have kids either. Rather, they go for ski trips, winter vacations in Mexico, or install jacuzzis in their spacious backyards. They take classes. They love learning how to cook Thai curries and drinking Chardonnay and skydiving and climbing Mt. Kilimanjaro. They both have full-time jobs that take up way too much of their time but are sort of fulfilling in an overstressed, global economy kind of way. Besides, they have to work just to be able to do things like own a home—in lots of cities, two full-time jobs these days will just cover the monthly mortgage payment.

In fact, the White Guy is increasingly the last guy on the planet to mate at all, if you track the birth rates of Euro White Guy, or even worse, Russian White Guy, who is so busy becoming a nouveau riche oligarch, he has no interest whatsoever in replenishing that vast, cold, vegetable-less country with little baby Ruskies.

White guys' mating and nesting habits have been the subject of a large number of published studies, mostly—and probably not coincidentally—written by females trying to figure out how they managed to get all that education, raise the roof on that glass ceiling so that they earn just about as much as guys, have amazing careers their moms could have only dreamt about, then totally forgot to nest with someone other than their cat.

One such book that's not completely from the non-guy point of view is *He's Just Not That Into You*, which tries to answer the question of why women have such a hard time attracting lifelong mates, despite the fact that they have read every self-help book out there, followed "The Rules," lived a "Purpose Driven Life," and adhere closely to the *Seven Habits of Highly Effective People*. These are the women who ventured out into the world and didn't make the choices that their girlfriends made. These women had dreams. Some of them fulfilled their dreams, only to wake up and realize they were 38, had dreamt the wrong dreams and the clock was almost up.

The authors, Greg Behrendt and Liz Tuccillo, basically had this advice for women everywhere: if there's a guy out there who you're crazy about, but who isn't quite crazy about you, cut your losses and run.

A Few Little-Known Clues to the Inner Life of the W Guy

1. Relationship Statute of Limitations

If a guy doesn't take the plunge within about a year of getting engaged, it's probably an excellent bet that he won't be taking the plunge—ever. Sure, his career needs stability. Sure, he needs a little longer before he's ready to really settle down. Know what? Every guy alive needs a little longer before he's ready to really settle down. And the ones who just *can't wait* for their wedding day? Approach with extreme caution. These guys are genetic freaks.

2. Emotional Expiry Dates

Everyone is fond of pointing to the fact that guys have no biological clock to listen to, but what gets talked about far less is that white guys develop habits, and a white guys' habits can be harder to break than most women realize. Trust me. If you've ever ridden the D train to Yankee Stadium, there is always that one white guy, wearing a Yanks cap, dressed in a stupid Yankee T-shirt, listening to his Walkman, gripping his scorecard, listening to the pre-game show. That guy was me when I lived in New York. The ritual of baseball is a habit that a certain generation of white guy absolutely adores, but which everyone else—even white guys from other generations—simply doesn't get.

They don't understand that it's the habit of baseball that we fall in love with.

That's why white guys need to get married by thirty-five, or else they end up more in love with their habits than they are with you. It doesn't matter if they're handsome or ugly, rich or poor, short or six foot six. If a white guy manages to remain single beyond that benchmark age, pity the poor wife who tries to yank the earphones off his head in the middle of a May West Coast swing through Seattle.

3. The Beta Boyfriend

Maureen Dowd is a columnist for the *New York Times*. She's funny, angry, political and smart, unless you're Dick Cheney (Darth Cheney to Dowd). Then she's bitter, caustic and agenda-driven.

The only blind spot she seems to have is guys.

Although she has dated such fellow high achievers as Aaron "West Wing" Sorkin and Michael Zeta-Douglas (before he became a Zeta), the notes she keeps bringing back are that men feel threatened by high-achieving women, and would far rather date women younger, prettier and no threat to out-earn them, unless they are supermodels or sitcom stars.

The *Globe and Mail*'s Ian Brown, a fiftysomething senior features writer himself who would make a good match for Dowd if he wasn't already married, wrote a column in response to Dowd. He conducted a highly informal survey of pals in his age bracket and found that they would have no problem being in a relationship with a woman who achieved more, earned more and generally displaced them as the primary income in the family.

Of course, his survey involved Canadian guys, the Beta W People of the Universe.

The truth is that Ms. Dowd might be onto something. I know, because I was one of those threatened, beta boyfriends she wrote about.

The High Achieving Woman and the Playwright

I met J at a Mexican restaurant on Second Avenue in the East Village of Manhattan. She was kind of spunky, cute, smart and precise. She was a former corporate attorney in her early thirties who was enrolled in Writer's Boot Camp. She was writing a screenplay. She also had a backstory that involved Winnipeg, and we knew a few of the same people. We had some margaritas, some Mary Anne's Mexican and told the Winnipeggers out with us that night a few New York horror stories that made me feel more like a New Yorker and less like a Winnipegger.

CUT TO:

August, 1993. I have sublet my apartment for a month to go sailing in British Columbia when I find out from my sailor friend that he's been audited and found wanting by the Canadian tax authorities. The sailing trip is cancelled. I'm sitting in Toronto, about to embark on a cross-country journey to begin my sailing trip, and now all of a sudden I have no home, at least not until September.

So I call J. We have been dating a little since June. Not a lot, but a little. Had a few good laughs. Then I went to a summer theatre conference in the Catskills for two weeks. One day she calls me.

"I just got offered a job as an entertainment lawyer for the coolest independent film lawyer in town," she says. "It only pays half of the corporate gig, but I know him from there. He's a cool guy, and my hours are set. I won't be coming home at ten at night. So I said, let's give it a try. To tell the truth, my screenplay sucks."

So now I was dating a lawyer, not a struggling screenwriter.

From Toronto, I tell her how I'm homeless for the next month.

"You can stay with me," she says. "I'm at work all day anyways. The only thing is that you have to share the space with my cat."

I stayed fourteen months.

Not only that, but J took her landlords to court for illegally over-charging her rent for the previous two or three years, and they paid her $8,000 to drop the suit, because if the court finds in favour of the tenant in New York City, the landlord pays triple damages— and the landlord had no case.

So, I start out dating a struggling screenwriter. I end up living in an East Village one-bedroom that costs $200 a month. J loves to go to good restaurants—and she buys. All she wants is company. She loves writers.

What's wrong with this picture?

Me. I am.

Because suddenly, my world changes.

In so many ways, it is the perfect scenario for a Writer Guy— and any guy who wants to be Writer Guy, for that matter. J wants to get married. She earns a living. She's indie as hell. Anything I make will be gravy. (We usually stuff my weekend earnings into the freezer to use as petty cash while the bills and rent come out of her chequing account.)

One night, we're walking home and she goes, "They say the best way for a child to learn a second language is for someone to speak to them exclusively in that language, so I was wondering if you prefer a Japanese or Spanish nanny?" [1]

That's a little jarring.

Another time, about a year into the thing, I catch her sitting by the window, gazing out at the backyard of Café Orlin, which is strung with party lights to make it feel festive.

---

1. J speaks Japanese, having spent a year of her law studies there.

"What are you thinking?" I ask.

"I have no problems," she says. "So I'm trying to anticipate what problems my kids might have."

Okay, she had a few lawyerly quirks.

The thing finally ended. It ended for me the night she asked me the question about what language I preferred that the nanny who was going to raise our hypothetical future child should speak. I just couldn't make that leap. Of course, a lot of guys couldn't. J probably didn't handle that too well. She was a planner type. I was a weekend-waiter/Off-Off-Broadway-playwright type. There was no word for "plan" in my vocabulary.

But I know I couldn't stand the fact, on some fundamental, male ego sort of level, that I was just the petty cash in the freezer. I would take a weekend a month off from my restaurant so we could go for a weekend in the country, or to fly to New Orleans or Santa Fe.

It bugged me. That's not how guys are wired. We would go out with friends, who were mostly other lawyers. In fact, they were mostly other gay lawyers and their boyfriends. One of the lawyers was practically a judge. And they all had boyfriends who were sort of artsy, cuter than they were. And that's what I was: the cute, artsy boyfriend. Beta Boyfriend. And I *hated* it.

Hated it so much, I did what very few New Yorkers will do, under even the worst duress: walked out of a rent-controlled, $200 a month one-bedroom apartment in the East Village with nothing planned. I mean, that's just not done. Furthermore, I had no social security number, no credit history and a part time job as a weekend waiter. Unless I was trying to get a flight back to Palookaville, I was committing Manhattanicide.

Honestly, the only Alpha Male thing I ever did during my relationship with J was to walk out on her. And her apartment.

The thing of it is, women are necessary. They're the ones who give birth to the next generation.

Guys aren't. It kind of sucks.

A few years ago, a woman asked, "What do men fear most?"

I thought about it. Commitment? Death? Being fat? Alone? Poor? A life of nine to five? A Leafs fan?

Then, remembering J, I said, "Feeling unnecessary."

Ten Emotional Sub-Species of White Guys

1. The Number Cruncher. Semi-autistic white males who are better at logarithms than conversation. These people run the world. They need a hug.

2. Emotionally Damaged White Guy. Someone hurt him—and he needs to get even. These guys either want to run the world or blow it up.

3. The Beta Boyfriend. I have no problems with your career coming first until I leave you. These people are go-along, get-along, until they aren't.

4. I'm in Control White Guy, AKA Leave Everything to Me White Guy. Trust me. I'll make this work. These guys have an answer for every question. Every question. Think about that.

5. Wealth Management White Guy. I know I'm not much to look at, but wait'll you catch a glimpse of my account summaries. These people know more than most about tipping hotel support staff.

6. Marries the First Girl He Has Sex With White Guy. That was *unbelievable.* Marry me?

7. Pursuit of Excellence White Guy. I only want the best. I'll call you. There's not really much excellent about these people except their opinion of themselves. See Interlude B.

8. No Friends White Guy. There's work. There's the wife. There's the kids. There's the game on TV. There's the little side project in order to bring home a little spare cash. What there *aren't* any of are friends.

9. Many Moves White Guy. Working on his thirteenth home in fourteen years. In some exurban paradise, just off the interstate,

with great access to the airport, which is great for all the business trips he has to take. Don't get too comfortable. As soon as you do, he has to move again.

10. Swinger White Guy. Monogamy is unnatural. As soon as we acknowledge that, we really begin to get in touch with ourselves. There's an orgy at the Anderson's Friday night.

Chapter Summary

The White Guy is notorious for not feeling his feelings—or anyone else's, for that matter. This produces a lot of friction everywhere on the planet.

THE QUEST
FOR AUTHENTICITY

THE DEEP, DARK secret of us white guys is that we don't really
have one.

We haven't overcome a lot of historical obstacles, although
"winter" ought to count for something.

We own pretty much everything—even a chunk of Oprah's show.

We aren't secretly gay, although we sometimes wish we were
because gay guys are so funny, so cut, so groomed, so prosperous, so
of-the-moment. Okay, maybe we're a little gay, but basically we still
believe, deep down, that if we could just accidentally-on-purpose
run into Scarlett Johansson or Jessica Alba or Halle Berry in the non-
fiction section of Barnes and Noble, we could get her to fall in love
with us. That's a lot of things—deluded, for one—but not very gay.

We aren't terribly oppressed, although you might hear differ-
ently from Career Academic White Guy trying to become chair
of the department after his third glass of white wine at the next
faculty reception.

Collectively, we're afraid of non-white guys, even though *we* are the most violent guys in history, perfectly willing to try to eliminate entire races if they get on our nerves enough. If anyone ought to feel very, very afraid, it's not us; it's everyone else.

OWING TO HIS geographic proximity to American White Guy, no one feels more inauthentic than Canadian White Guy—a guy like me. The truth is that the most truly authentic experience a lot of white guys have had over the years is listening to all the horrible things that have happened to the non-white, non-guys of the world out there coping with global chaos, much of it the fallout from centuries of white guys coming up with really, really bad ideas about what to do next.

That isn't easy. I'm not sure there's a book in that sort of thing, though.

However, my brother-in-law—another white guy from Winnipeg, named Kevin—and I did discover something inauthentic Canadian white guys could do to create a veneer of authenticity on our lives: marry non-white Baltimore-raised actresses who happen to be bona-fide sisters.

After all, look around at the world: every morning we wake up to one more global crisis, frequently the result of a culture clash, where one culture says one thing, another culture completely misinterprets it as an act of aggression, and then the war is on.

Try that every day at home, and you'll get the idea.

Ironically, non-white, non-guys like Mel also have their own crisis of authenticity. She has a little voice in her head that follows her where ever she goes, admonishing her about not being an authentic black person, because she grew up wishing Christopher Plummer in *The Sound of Music* was her dad, went to college in Vermont and married me. Barack Obama, who had an African dad, is accused by a lot of African-Americans of not being black enough. Dutch political writer Ayaan Hirsi Ali is viewed by a lot of Muslims as an inauthentic Muslim woman with a crush on Western rational thought.

The truth of the matter is that lots of people besides white guys have crises of authenticity these days. It's practically just another way of saying, "global economy."

One of the strongest bonds I have with Melanee is that she feels like an inauthentic black person and as a Canadian, I am the poster child for the inauthentic white guy—and together we are raising a son who is Canadian, American, white, non-white and kind of short.

Send the therapy bills to my publisher.

So when you read about the latest scandal about some white guy author lying about his past in order to make it sound worse than it really was, ask yourself: is this man a liar, or simply an anxious, inauthentic white guy? If it's the latter, give him a hug, tell him it's okay and hand him a copy of this book.

Ten Most Inauthentic White Guys of All-Time

10. Charles Bukowski. Poet. Mailman. Drunk. Perfect. So what if he started out a middle-class kid in L.A.?

9. Bob Dylan. Ramblin' hobo, blowin' in the wind, Mr. Tambourine Man like a rolling stone guy, claimed he rode the rails to New York with Woodie Guthrie. Actually, he was born Robert Zimmerman, the child of a hardware store owner in Minnesota. Who wants to hear about the meaning of life from a hardware store owner's son?

8. Tony Blair. Visionary Labour leader, or ambitious politician who actually just wanted to be liked by Americans? You be the judge, history.

7. Pete Seeger. Folksinger guy who borrowed quite a bit of the man-of-the-people bit. But hey, so did Joe Stalin. And I like those hats.

6. The Strokes. East Village punk revivalists led by scion of fashion and art world who are about as punk as Camilla Parker Bowles.

5. Kim Philby. Upper-Middle-Class British Empire White Guy turned Soviet spy. Quite a hedge hater.

4. Kenny Chesney. Bon vivant, good ole boy country music star with a dash of Jimmy Buffett island-hopping—or New Nashville nightmare? You be the judge.

3. Thomas Friedman. *New York Times* world affairs columnist. Man-of-the-people columnist guy with billionaire wife. I like how he won't cut off his porn star moustache.

2. James Frey. Pseudo-memoirist who lied to Oprah. The guy is dead to me.

1. George W. Bush. Texan. Brush-clearer *extraordinaire*. Man of the big-belt-buckle people. James Frey finds this guy unbearably fake.

Interlude Summary

Many white guys feel our lives lack authenticity, which we compensate for either by appropriating the cultural experiences of non-white and/or non-guys, or by making stuff up.

WHITE GUY CULTURE

. . .

Part One:
White Guy (Unpopular) Culture

BEFORE THERE WAS YouTube, text messaging, iPods, Facebook, content on demand, and DVD players in mini-vans to mute the kids on road trips up the New Jersey Turnpike, there was something called culture, with a capital C.

I don't mean the 1990s, although once in a while I do long for the snail mail era.

I mean, way before there was even electricity, there was Culture. I'm talking about centuries and centuries back, during those tweener centuries no one ever really thinks about except fantasy novelists.

Culture was what civilized W people had. They didn't have showers. They didn't have cars (did the guys sit around bragging about the size of their horses?). So what if they owned slaves? They had Culture! Whatever poor people did in their spare time—clog dancing in the mud, keeping time on tree stumps, wailing their sorrows in verse—could hardly be called culture. At least not until several centuries later, when W people realized there was some serious coin to be made off all that stuff, particularly if you got young, attractive W people to act as if it was their culture, too.

Some Other Kinds of Old-School, AKA Classical Culture

Symphony orchestras, opera and ballet continue to exist in many major metropolitan areas across the world, much to the surprise of just about everyone, because just about everyone doesn't care about any of them. Live theatre continues to exist as well—and the most popular playwright is still William Shakespeare, a white guy who had a way with words and wrung a lot of laughs out of cross-dressing. He also died about four centuries ago, which tells you just about everything you need to know about live theatre.

The All-Pro W Painters (and One Sculptor)

10. Pablo Picasso. Short, mercurial Spaniard who reinvented perspective and sired a daughter who sells perfume.
9. Rembrandt. Anyone know this guy's first name?
8. Michelangelo. Tended towards the over-the-top, but that will happen when they ask you to paint the ceiling of the Sistine Chapel.
7. Andy Warhol. Soup cans have not been the same since Andy.
6. Jasper Johns. American White Guy stars 'n' stripes painter extraordinaire.
5. Monet. Spawned the entire French postcard industry with his picturesque depictions of the Gallic countryside.
4. Gustav Klimt. Austrian white guy who had a way with glitter.
3. J.M.W. Turner. British Empire White Guy who really had a knack for portraits of sailing ships in storms dumping slaves into the water, and other bleak stuff.
2. Vincent Van Gogh. Even an ear short of a headset, he could paint a swirling sky like nobody before or since.
1. Auguste Rodin. French sculptor guy who is responsible for many of the best sculpture gardens you'll ever sit in and sip a Tall Americano.

Part Two: White Guy (Popular) Culture

The movies, music, TV and video games all make up popular white guy culture, although frankly, with this stuff, the emphasis is just as much on the popular as it is on the culture part. This set of priorities has allowed us to turn a blind eye whenever necessary to aspects of culture that might prove unpopular, like the truth. When the truth gets popular, we'll be the first to cash in on that, too.

The Movies: A Memoir

The first movie I saw, at a drive-in when I was about five, was *Swiss Family Robinson*, a Disney film about a family of W People who get stranded on a desert island and are forced to adapt to life without technological convenience, anonymous banking or Swiss chocolate. Well, as it turns out, the Swiss Family Robinson are the sort of highly efficient, innovative, over-achieving castaways that make Gilligan, the Skipper, Mary Anne, Ginger, Tom Hanks and that volleyball Wilson look like heroin-shooting slackers. The Swiss Family Robinson build pulleys and tree houses, troughs that allow them to catch fish and fresh water, and just basically make the deserted island adapt to them, rather than vice versa. When faced with an external threat—pirates—they invent coconut bombs, which they catapult at the pirates.

Eventually, it ends well for the Swiss Family Robinson. They tame nature rather than regress back to their primitive selves. They acquire enviable tans rather than skin cancer, ripped bodies that make one wonder where they hid the Soloflex and, most surprising of all, good hair instead of an unmanageable tangle. Best of all, they bond as a family unit, rather than forming cliques and plotting until they eat each other.

They are W People in paradise.[1]

Interestingly, the other movie on that first double feature was *The Love Bug*, another Disney film. Only *The Love Bug* is a

---

1. Memo to self: *The Seven Habits of Highly Effective Castaways?* Query editors.

Volkswagen with human feelings! Not only is it cute, but it cares about its owner, played by Dean Jones, the un–Kurt Russell, a nerdy everyman no one, aside from his car, cares about.

I can't remember the plot of *The Love Bug*, but I loved it nevertheless. I loved watching a world where technology cares, we're all in it together, and, most importantly, it all works out in the end. Coming hard off a film where nature bends to the will of W People, where families that castaway together stay together, where a little human can-do turns being shipwrecked into a remarkable opportunity, it was a perfect introduction to the popular culture of white guys.

While the popular culture of white guys shape-shifts a little from year to year depending on what Steve Jobs and the guys at Pixar are up to, it really hasn't changed a lot over the centuries. It has always been, and always will be, about heroes and evil villains.

He might come in different shapes (aliens, Nazis), sizes (giants, worms), colours (non-white guy) or spiritual beliefs (non-white savage Muslim guy), but the evil villain is basically the same guy, over and over and over, played by a character actor who wonders whatever prompted him to move to stinking L.A. just so that he could set his race back three decades playing pimps, drug lords or crazy crack 'hos.

While people in the movie industry tend to think the popular culture of white guys was invented by Robert McKee at one of his overpriced, three-day screenwriting seminars, it was actually created by Aristotle, Ancient Greek White Guy, who invented the whole heroes and villains bit—or at least got the screen credit for it.

Needless to say, Ancient Greek publicists really possessed the gift of the gab, so Aristotle's legend continued to grow, right through the Roman Ages, the Muslim Caliphate, the Middle, Dark and Medium-Rare Ages, through the Renaissance, Restoration Hardware and Enlightenment, all the way up to approximately 2002, when Aristotle was supplanted in popular lore by Charlie

Kaufman, the greatest screenwriter since Billy Wilder—but that's for another book.

As I was saying, white guy popular culture is about storytelling, and let's be frank, can we? The one story white guys love to tell is the one where white guys win.

Not only that, but in the process of winning, white guys demonstrate an array of the highest sort of human qualities. White guys in popular culture are generally portrayed as altruistic forces, real team players and good listeners. We are decisive but fair, tougher than we look but reluctant to use physical force, in control of our emotional impulses rather than out to kick Muslim ass, kind, compassionate, omniscient and benevolent. A typical Hollywood hero is a handsome white man with soulful eyes, great hair and a hell of a winsome smile, who overcomes mind-boggling physical obstacles, tiptoes over some vexing emotional obstacle, like making an emotional commitment or hating his dad, and does all this at maximum warp speed, with a rapier wit, an air of nonchalance and a willingness to take the occasional timeout for some balls-to-the-wall love making.

In short, we are Christopher Plummer in *The Sound of Music*: single dads raising wonderful child stars and falling in love with the help—21-year-old Julie Andrews—even as the Nazis descend on our beautiful home.[2]

While the decades change, bringing with them new screen heroes—Jimmy Stewart, Clark Gable, John Wayne, Gary Cooper, Bogie, Rock Hudson, Dick Burton, Peter O'Toole, Chuck Heston, Gregory Peck, Jack Lemmon, Jack Nicholson, Pacino, De Niro, Hoffman, Cruise, Eastwood, Arnold, Stallone, Redford, Newman, Beatty, Michael Douglas, Richard Gere, all the way up to Clooney, Pitt and Damon—the type of guy played doesn't really shift

---

2. Note to editor: were the Nazis white? How can they be evil villains and white? *Ed:* good question. Ask Günter Grass.

all that much, at least not in the big studio movies. They might gain weight, grow beards, learn accents, have absurd affairs with insanely sexy co-stars, live in villas or the Beverly Hills Hotel or a loft in Tribeca or Montparnasse, but at the end of the day, they're basically white guys there to save the day—or, as Melanee likes to call them, Big Daddy White Men.

There are different visions of white guy life, depending on the available light where you grew up. If you grew up in rural Sweden, you turn into Ingmar Bergman and see Death prancing through the forest. If you grew up in Italy, you turn into Federico Fellini and life is a surreal circus filled with sex, food and Marcello Mastroianni. If you grew up in Little Italy in Lower Manhattan, you turn into Marty Scorsese and life is filled with Catholic guilt, well-dressed gangsters and spasms of horrifying violence. And Bobby De Niro. If you grew up in Victoria, B.C., like Atom Egoyan, you make slow-moving masterpieces of alienation and compassion, which, when you stop and think about it, perfectly describes what it's like to be Canadian.

Non-White Guy's role in the popular culture of white guys has shifted over the years, too, but basically, non-white guy has always existed to play either the evil villain or the amiable sidekick who helps the hero achieve his goal.

The weirdest thing about Hollywood is the contradiction between its advertising, which is very of-the-moment, in-your-face, sexy and irresistible, and the actual content it promotes, which tends to be about a decade behind the rest of the popular culture. Hollywood movies are the oil tankers of popular culture; they're big and expensive and require a lot of lead-time. However, times change, even on oil tankers. It may change at the speed of a glacier melting in Hollywood, but in case you haven't noticed, those glaciers are almost gone.

Result: in 2007, the biggest movie star in the world is Will Smith, and Denzel Washington isn't far behind—despite the long-held Hollywood conventional wisdom that non-white guys can't open a film overseas.

Ten Whitest Movies Ever Made

10. Every Tom Hanks romantic comedy. He's nice, non-threatening, kind of boring-looking but secretly a good whistler.[3] He's not your dream lover, but he'll make a hell of a husband.
9. Every film featuring Harvey Keitel full frontal nudity. We refer of course to that troika: *The Bad Lieutenant, The Piano* and 1978's *Fingers*, in all of which he dropped trou' in the name of expressing himself. Hey Harvey, who do you think you are, Kate Winslet? Put some clothes on, man.
8. *Birth of a Nation.* The heroes are the KKK, who restore order to the South following the chaos of the Civil War. Result: mega-hit that grossed $10 million, in 1915 dollars. Also provoked the occasional riot and had a sixty-year run as a recruiting film for the Klan.
7. *Dances With Wolves.* A frontier white guy in the nineteenth century gets put in charge of wiping out the Indians, and instead becomes one. Kevin Costner's last, great Hollywood moment, before he discovered (big, expensive, apocalyptic, incomprehensible) water movies, then watched his career as a movie star wash away with them.
6. *Metropolitan.* Concerned with white people on the isle of Manhattan who have good manners, a keen sense of hierarchy and seethe with sexual desire as they try to make sense of life in complete sentences.
5. *Fargo.* Murder mystery set in the wintery-plains states, starring Francis McDormand, William H. Macy and Steve Buscemi, three of the whitest people in the history of movies.

---

3. Holden Caulfield, the hero of *The Catcher in the Rye*, said not to feel sorry for boring guys because secretly they might be good whistlers.

4. *Taxi Driver*. An alienated cabbie, dismayed by the way his beloved New York City has changed, vows to clean the scum off the streets.[4]
3. *It's a Wonderful Life*. It is if you're white, anyways.
2. *The Last Samurai*. Only a W person like Tom Cruise could invent a movie that's an ode to the Japanese samurai warrior and then decide to make it a movie where the W samurai guy lives in the end. Holy culture clash, Batman.
1. *The Big Chill*. A lot of W people who went to college together in the '60s have a reunion weekend, where they reminisce in some-one's cottage about their dead friend, failed relationships, celebri-ties and how they meant to change the world but sort of lost track of that. Yes—it's the biopic of all W people in a nutshell. (And they cut Costner's part completely—he played the dead friend.)

Music

The White Guy is fond of music, enjoying it in the car, the elevator and anywhere he can plug in an iPod and create a wall of sound between himself and the rest of the world.

The exact origins of White Guy music are vague, although there is rumoured to have been a folk festival shortly following the first harvest, in Canaan around 1000 BC with (legend has it) Pete Seeger as the headliner, singing his number one hit, "My God is Better Than Your God," although it's totally possible that's just malicious web gossip.

Music first became popular because the caves that earliest white guy lived in had great acoustics. The first known percussion-ist was the fire starter, who cut a nice beat scraping a couple flints together trying to ignite a spark. The first known vocalist was the

---

4. There's not much doubt Scorsese is talking non-white guy when he talks scum, although here the part of non-white pimp guy is played by Harvey Keitel with surprising effectiveness. Unless of course there was a subclass of pimp white guy we didn't know about in mid-'70s New York City.

guy sitting next to him, who caught an errant spark in the foot and hollered out in pain.

Music was popular through the eras dominated by kings and queens. Kings and queens enjoyed a good tune at night after another day of heavy lifting of food to their grills.[5] They also encouraged the musicians of the court to do side gigs for peasants, as music had a pleasant soothing quality that kept the peasants from revolting against the kingdom, at least until Marie Antoinette and her cake cracks.

It was during this period that a lot of the top piano players of the day came around, particularly Mozart, who, if history is to be believed, had quite a head of hair on him. Mozart was the Wayne Gretzky of piano players, though he was also famous for overwriting.

Meanwhile, Over in the States, a Century or Two Later . . .

While non-white guy was having a miserable experience of it down south, poor, white, free guy was out West in the U.S., sitting around a fire hoping there were no Indians out beyond the campfire's light waiting with sharpened tomahawks for him to doze off so they could remove his scalp. This produced the earliest country music, which experts call the pre-Nashville sound.

Country Music White Guy never lost track of the need for heroes and evil villains in his narratives, but mostly his songs concerned themselves with loneliness. He might have been white, a guy and free, but that was about it for upside. Half his teeth were missing, he had the worst sunburn ever and *hated* the dry, lonely, empty, dangerous, hot, nutritionally deficient desert, although it *did* beat spending the rest of your life paying back a bank note on a business gone bad back in St. Louis. (And the stars sure were pretty at night.)

---

5. "Grill" is radio host Jim Rome's term for "face."

In the cities, Jazz White Guy rode buses and played gigs and chased chicks. A lot of American non-white guys—some of the greatest musicians the land has produced, such as Chick Webb and Louis Armstrong—also rode buses and played gigs, although there was always the small problem of locating a hotel at the end of the long drive, because hotels didn't welcome non-white guys in many parts of the U.S. until the Supreme Court forced them to.

(Note that seamless historical transition, where Jazz W Guy suddenly materializes out of nowhere. Actually, those non-W guys playing jazz led to Jazz W Guy playing jazz in all the places where club owners wouldn't hire non-W guys, like Chick Webb and Louis Armstrong, who were only geniuses. Who invented jazz? Not us.)

This oddly parallel universe—white jazz guy on his bus, non-white jazz guy on his bus—continued for many years, until Benny Goodman became a bandleader and began to hire non-white guys to play in it. Because he was Benny Goodman, superstar, all the club owners were too afraid to point out what he was doing, which resulted in music becoming de-segregated, quite a bit ahead of the rest of white guy society, which saw no reason to upset the apple cart.

While the White Guy excelled at earlier, more melodious forms of music, he didn't hesitate to take credit for anything else interesting that came down the pike. The Beatles and the Rolling Stones, and before them Elvis and the early rockers, loved African-American R&B and Soul—they just adapted it to white tastes, and made a killing. Benny Goodman was a white guy who was good at jazz. Eminem is a white guy who is good at hip hop. David Byrne is a white guy who is pretty good at Brazilian samba. So when does borrowing end and stealing start? Or does music just belong to everyone?

Mel grew up in a single-mom household in Baltimore with three brothers and sisters, watching TV. Whenever a white singer or band came on, Mel's mom would point at the TV screen and say, "they stole that from black people!"

Quincy Jones bought a TV pilot off of me once. We met at his house, which was way up atop Bel Air Road in one of the most exclusive parts of L.A. You can bet not too many *jazz* musicians who came of age in the '50s and '60s are Q's neighbours.

I asked him how he did it. How did he end up mega-rich, when so many musicians end up penniless?

He wouldn't sell his copyrights. He told stories of black musicians being dangled from hotel windows by their ankles by thugs hired by white record publishers until they gave up the copyrights to their songs for relative pittances. Somewhere along the way, he found a way to hang on to his—I'm not sure how, he's kind of short—but he just moved into an even bigger estate up atop the same road!

Of course, it didn't hurt that Q produced *Thriller*, the top selling record of all-time.

The truth, though, is that there are far more musicians who end up with nothing than end up loaded like Q. There were lots of great non-white guy musicians during the first seventy-five years of the twentieth century whose musical stylings were appropriated, adapted or just plain stolen.

Take the '70s, the Disco era. Remember that? Cocaine was just good, energizing fun. Sex was just sex. And music was meant to be danced to. One of the most popular bands was Boney M., who sang about the rivers of Babylon and Rasputin, lover of the Russian queen. They sold millions of records and were on every radio station, worldwide.

The Boney M. on the record cover were four black people. The sound was a little more difficult to identify. It wasn't quite R&B or funk. It was vaguely Euro Beatific and the vocals were a highly annoying falsetto.

Turns out the singer was a German guy named Frank Farian, who loved disco beat music but figured out early in the game that no one wanted to see a disco band led by a less-than-attractive white guy. So he hired four non-white people—one man and three women—to become the face of Boney M. Then he wrote and recorded all the songs and dubbed in his whining falsetto.

And then, Frank became rich as Boney M. soared up the charts in Europe, the U.K. and the U.S. (although they soared a little lower in the States.).

Eventually, the people who played Boney M. on record covers were allowed to sing the songs themselves on tour, and eventually they even kicked Frank out of the band he had invented.

It's hard to blame the non-white people for wanting to kick Frank out of the band (he eventually cashed in on hip hop as the voice behind Milli Vanilli). Lots of them were denied access to audiences thanks to segregation, or grossly underpaid or simply had their music stolen from them by a music industry that was full of pirates before the term "musical piracy" was even invented.

As recently as the early '80s, MTV had to be threatened with a boycott in order to get them to play videos featuring non-white artists. MTV went on air on August 1, 1981, but it wasn't until March 31, 1983, that they played a video by a non-white guy artist: "Beat It," by Michael Jackson. Of course, MTV suits said it wasn't about race, it was about what audiences wanted. And then, perhaps faced with a boycott by Jackson's record label, they gave in and started playing Jackson's videos, which turned out to be exactly what audiences wanted.

Maybe they thought we weren't ready to watch music videos by non-white guys. (Think of the ruined hamstrings after a bunch of loaded white guys tried to imitate Michael's dance moves.)

These days, you would think this sort of conversation would have sort of died down. After all, plenty of non-white people are the biggest stars in the recording industry: Kanye West, Beyoncé, John Legend, JayZ and 50 Cent.

But then we're back in Baltimore, for Thanksgiving. It's 2007. We're driving through neighbourhood's where Melanee and her big sister Melissa used to live, and they start talking about Amy

Winehouse, the British R&B singer, who has carved a name out for herself by pretty much mimicking the singing style of an old black blues lady, except she's young, white and British.

"I'm not saying it's appropriation, but couldn't girlfriend add something to the sound?" Melissa says.

Sasha Frere-Jones is the music critic for *The New Yorker*. Recently, Sasha started a fight when he complained that indie rock has gotten too white, that its lost all its rythym, that somewhere along the way, Indie Rocker White Guy stopped borrowing from black people—and now music is worse off for it. Now, he wrote, indie rock has gotten too white for words—or actually it's become nothing but the words, which are clever, arch and ironic, but somehow the music itself has lost its flavour, the stuff that made the Stones so great.

One of the main bands he singled out, too, was Arcade Fire, one of those cool Montreal bands who kind of sound like U2, only without trying to save the world.

All of which leaves me... confused. Sounds a bit like white guys can't win when they pay homage to non-white guy music (Amy Winehouse) and they can't win when they don't (Arcade Fire).

What are you gonna do?

I wrote Sasha Frere-Jones an email.

All things considered, I asked, did white guys steal rock and roll? He wrote back one word: *yep*.

Ten Whitest Songs Ever

10. "Play That Funky Music (White Boy)." If you don't know any, some death metal will do.
9. "God Save the Queen." The theme song for the British Empire. (Not to be confused with the Sex Pistols cover version, which has different lyrics but is also quite Caucasian.)
8. "If I Had a Million Dollars." Barenaked Ladies tune white guys hum their babies to sleep with.

7. "A Whiter Shade of Pale." Just thinking out loud here, but what could be whiter than pale? Membership to Yale's Order of Skull and Bones? Mormon marriage? Rush Limbaugh's core demographic?

6. "White Christmas." Why does Christmas gotta be white?

5. "White Wedding." Billy Idol's finest musical moment summed up an entire era.

4. "Sultans of Swing." Dire Straits song about a bunch of jazz-playing English white guys in London.

3. "All My Heroes Are Cowboys." You'd have to be white and a guy to understand.

2. "God Bless America." That was before God found out about Iraq.

1. "Pretty Fly (For a White Guy!)." Hey—fly white guys happen. Just not very often. And when they do happen, it calls for a song.

Television

Television is the thing in the corner of every house in the world. It is cheap to buy a television, considering.[6] There are tens of thousands of hours of television programming out there, floating around in the firmament, available to program directors of television stations just about anywhere.

While there are lots of shows featuring non-white guys in non-American locations, there is nothing quite like American television, particularly if you are living in some dirt-poor part of the world, looking for a reason to look forward to the rest of your hard, dirt-poor, unjust life.

American television is the realm of the empathetic, patriarchal, patient, employed, prosperous white guy dad. He's in shape—or at least else he's loveably out of shape—has good hair, a sense of humour and a life any dirt poor non-white guy anywhere would die for. Let's face it: American television creates a lot of expectations about America that America can't quite live up to.

---

6. Considering you can pass a lifetime watching it.

I grew up in Canada, watching American television. In my young, impressionable mind, there were only two kinds of places: places that were on television, and places that weren't.

Winnipeg was never on American television. Places that were, such as Devil's Lake, Fargo, Moorhead and—most exotically—Minneapolis, seemed positively Parisian by comparison.

It was kind of a bummer.

When you think you come from a place television forgot, it tends to inflate the places television remembers in your own imagination. Growing up living next to American television was the cultural equivalent of growing up living next to Chernobyl. American television completely shaped my sense of reality, or maybe misshaped it. But that's the power of television. Television was where your funny, kind friends lived, even if you didn't have any. Television was full of days unlike any other. Television sought, and obtained, emotional resolutions to very vexing problems. Television discovered a measure of justice in the world, right at fifty-eight minutes after the hour, in time for the hero to make a detached, witty observation about life before cutting to the sponsor's message.

Television was neat, tidy and fun, and all of its heroes were white guys.

Canada is great at peacekeeping. We rock at hockey. We rule curling. We make great game show hosts, news anchors and folksingers.

Canada sucks at television. Big time.

. . . .

MEL'S DEEP THOUGHT

(Another in an occasional series of interruptions to the narrative flow)

No. 3: A TOPSY-TURVY WORLD

. . .

IMAGINE THIS: You are a nice, hardworking, middle class white man from Western Canada. You wake up one day to find yourself transposed to a reverse universe. You open your morning paper while you smell the aroma of your (white) coffee, and the paper is full of the usual comments by corporate leaders, government officials and entertainers. But look closely. There are black faces everywhere! A black woman stands on the presidential podium. Black men—those really tall, really dark, really scary basketball types—are leading congress, brokering mergers and inventing vaccines. Turn the page. More black people: black men, black women. And some Asians, too, way more than you're used to, as well as Indians, Latinos, Pakistanis, First Nations. They are everywhere. The only time you catch a glimpse of a white face is in the city section, where somebody who could be your cousin is walking into a jailhouse, hands cuffed behind his back, a blank stare hiding his feelings.

Astounded, you turn on the TV. Not only is Oprah black, but the cast of *Friends, Frasier,* all but the reality shows, which are full of the lowest common denominator of White America. The one thing that hasn't changed is the music. It's all black, of course, but gone are any references to Britney, Elvis or the Stones. Or if they are noted, they are done so by some patronizing talk show host who sounds like he's talking to small children: "That's nice. How you copied Muddy Waters. And Bessie Smith. And Little Richard. Keep it up. You might just stumble onto something original."

End of Deep Thought.

. . . .

American Television White Guys

Archie Bunker, Hawkeye, Rockford, Lou Grant, Murray, Ted, Dick Van Dyke, JR, Bobby Ewing, Sam the Bartender, Norm, Frasier, Niles, Chandler, Ross, Tony Soprano, Paulie Walnuts, Christopher, Larry David, Mr. Big, Aidan, George, Kramer, Jerry, Ray Romano, his brother, Jack on 24, Bob Newhart, every CSI guy, Detective Briscoe, Columbo, Kojak, Captain Furillo, Magnum, Johnny, Dave, Jay, Jimmy, Conan, Jon (where'd that h go, Jon?), Simon Cowell, Bill O'Reilly, Dan Rather, Jennings, Brokaw, Brian Williams,

Anderson, Dan Patrick, Keith Olbermann, Bill Maher, Regis, Alex Trebek, Vinnie Barbarino, Arnold Horschak, Mr. Kotter, the Fonz, Richie, Mr. Cunningham, Ralph Malph, Potsie—and I could fill a book. American television has been one continuous fifty-year-long infomercial for the white guy.

I can't imagine what it's like to be a non-white, non-guy growing up in America, wondering what happened to your life. Well, I sort of can, since Mel tells me.

She lived all over Baltimore, with three siblings and a single mom. It was hard, unstable and a struggle. Mel's family had education. Her mom got a degree in French. Her grandparents on her dad's side were teachers and high school principals back in the day when civil rights for non-white guys were just a rumour. Her uncle went to West Point and graduated from Harvard Business School.

None of which mattered much when it came to television.

Mel has one brother, her big brother, who was forced to play the dad in their family. It was not easy. He was a kid, not a dad. He shouldn't have had to grow up so fast. It damaged him. He had a lot of trouble handling the strain. Their dad left Mel's family and started a new one—with a white woman. Needless to say, W People were not high on the list of family likes.

Mel's big brother's favourite TV show was *The Courtship of Eddie's Father*.

If you can't have a benevolent, present dad in real life, you could always have Bill Bixby on American television. I loved Bill Bixby, too. He was a lot cooler than my dad, who had anger-management issues, money problems and three needy kids tugging on his leg when he came home from work.

Anyways, cut to years and years later. We live in Santa Monica, in the heart of Hollywood. I work at a production company, with a deal at ABC Television. Mel is an actor, who now acts on television. She goes to auditions. She gets cast in shows such as *Law & Order, Judging Amy,* 24 and *Everybody Loves Raymond*. It's always great, when you're a struggling actor, to get a gig, and the money can't be beat, but even as she learns to navigate the treacherous byways of Hollywood, Mel grows more and more irritated by it.

Script after script shows up at our door with parts for her. The only problem is that they're all the same part, every single one of them, or a variation on the same part: a crazy drug-addicted crack head single mom jailbird ghetto-fabulous gold-digging 'ho.

One day, she gets a call for a part. She's going straight to producers. That's basically Hollywood slang for, "The part is yours to lose, hon." The producers don't want to go through the process of auditioning that part; they want you. They know you, they've seen your work, and it works for them.

The part is of course, the crack 'ho from hell.

Mel comes home from her audition fuming.

"I blew it," she says. "I just talked too much. I showed them that I was educated. You could tell they didn't want to know that. They just want some gold-tooth wearin' (ghetto), booty-shakin' (bubble-butted), biz-natch (bitch) to conform to their (racist) stereotypes," she says. "That's every part I get offered. I went to Bennington. I'm thinking of getting a Masters, but do I ever get offered a part that bears even a vague relationship to *me*?"

When we watch TV, she points out all of the subtle ways in which Hollywood casts minority parts.

This basically involves watching any black female character on any TV show and chanting, "Weave-wearin', nose job–gettin', high-yella bitch!"

Say what?

Translation, for all the mystified Ws:

1. Weave: fake hair that African-Americans wear to give their hair the silky quality W People's hair has, because of the longstanding fear W People have had of crinkly, tightly wound, thick, dry non-W hair.

2. Nose job–gettin': The African nose is flatter and broader than the W's pointy beak. Even though most W's would say we don't notice noses to that degree, non-W, non-guy actresses would say, go look at every African-American actress who gets cast and count the nosejobs they got to make their noses look more like a W person's nose. Per capita, there are as many nose jobs among non-W actresses as there are boob jobs among blondes, which just goes to show you oppression knows no colour.

3. High-yella bitch: A derogatory name for a mulatto, usually spoken out of exasperation, because mulatto actresses book way more work than darker-skinned actresses.

I love *The West Wing*, but it gets on Mel's nerves. She doesn't like the Dulé Hill character, the non-white guy who plays an intern who ends up being a kind of presidential administrative assistant to Martin Sheen.

"For one thing, why did they have to cast it that way?" she asks, pointing out that Dulé Hill is sort of funny looking. "There's a thousand black men out there who look better than that bug-eyed fool," she says, "but they don't want to cast a black man who looks better than Josh and the rest of them. They don't want to cast a black man the President's daughter actually might stay with, so they cast this guy instead."

Second of all, she doesn't like it that his character's name is Charlie.

She calls it *"The White Wing."*

Anyways, things are changing—sort of. And you could pull out the casting of every show and probably get some statistics to show that television is more diverse than it used to be. But even when it is, when there's a show—generally a crime drama—featuring racially diverse casting, what's the one thing no one ever, and I mean ever, talks about?

That's why we need this book!

WHILE THEY HAVE numbered in the thousands, there are a few recognizable archetypal white guys on television that more or less define the medium:

Anchorman White Guy

He puts the world into context for everyone else. He has a good strong jaw, a prominent head of hair and a penetrating gaze. If you and your spouse were to die in a horrible plane crash, you would be relieved to have Anchorman White Guy raise your orphaned children.

Investigative White Guy

Investigative white guy is always a man in pursuit of What Really Happened. He's a truth anthropologist, out to set the record straight, even if it means running afoul of the people in power who are more interested in remaining in power than in finding out What Really Happened. Investigative White Guy is detail oriented, a good listener and sarcastic as hell. We are never shocked to discover that Investigative White Guy is alone in the world and has a couple failed marriages behind him, which doesn't taint him in any way, because as we all know deep down that people interested in What Really Happened weren't meant to co-exist with spouses in this world. He's quite a guy, and frequently works with an ethnic sidekick, which makes for quite a diverse, knowable, truth-loving world inside the television, does it not?

American Dad White Guy

Twenty-first century American Dad White Guy is perhaps best captured by Hal on *Malcolm in the Middle*. Played by Brian Cranston, Hal is underemployed, dead broke, overwhelmed by life, but willing to show up every day. He never really understood how much work kids were until they showed up at his door. He never gets any time to himself. He dresses horribly, in shirt sleeves and those pants my mom used to call "slacks." Above everything else, he is all about the family unit.

Sports Play-by-Play White Guy

He knows his sports, but never jokes about how sports don't really matter. Sports matter! They aren't simply entertainment, they're a rite of passage, a tradition passed between fathers and sons, an ancient ritual dating back thousands of years. Probably there was an ancient Greek play-by-play guy calling out the action when the rosy-fingered dawn spread its fingers and the dark ships set sail for Troy to get that damn Helen back from the Argonauts or whoever took her. (And we all know how soft Argonaut fans are.)

The archetypal Sports Play-by-Play White Guy is Fox Sports broadcaster Joe Buck, who is descended from a long line of Sports Play-by-Play W Guys. Although only about thirty-five, Buck appears, in voice, mannerism and worldview, to be sixty-seven. He adopts the perspective of a mythical Middle America, a place that existed on American television forty years ago but has been extinct for several decades now, unless you attend St. Louis Cardinals games.

The very best Sports Play-by-Play W Guy is Marv Albert. Albert is burdened by the fact that he is a New Yorker through and through, and there was also an unfortunate sex scandal about ten years ago, but hey, he wasn't married.

The truth of the matter is that a generation of white guys grew up listening to Sports Play-by-Play White Guy on the portable radio in bed as he called games, and thus Sports Play-by-Play White Guy has acquired a status in the hearts and minds of many white guys and non-white guys as probably the closest thing we have to a god.

Reality TV Host White Guy

While we tend to think of reality television as a very late twentieth-century creation, the godfather of the role is actually Ed Sullivan, who was, if not the very first Reality TV Host White Guy, then the first to become an icon. Since Ed Sullivan was before our time and we are not very terribly interested in trekking to the Museum of Broadcasting to view grainy old tape of the ugly bastard, let us move on to the twenty-first century incarnation, best exemplified by that *American Idol* duo, Ryan Seacrest and Simon Cowell.

Reality TV Host White Guy is attractive—and judgmental. He's funny yet supportive. He's us—somewhat detached from the goings-on, as we meet the reality show contestants and endure their painfully lame backstories as they attempt to build emotional support with their dime-store dreams. He would rather be on a movie shoot somewhere, or even doing a sitcom, but his agent assured him this hosting gig was high profile and will ultimately pay off farther down the road, so here he is, acting interested as the sad-sack parade carries on.

He's the face of contemporary television!

Ten Whitest Guys in Television History

1. Archie Bunker from *All In The Family*. He's white, he's declining, he's bitter, he's looking for someone to blame. He was us. Did we get any better? Maybe, but the shows about guys like us sure didn't.
2. Hawkeye Pierce from *M*A*S*H*. He's a doctor, he's a player, he's a patriot on his terms, he's funny, he's sleazy, but when push comes to shove, he's there. He's even a freaking patriot.
3. Andy Sipowicz from *NYPD Blue*. He's fat, he's married, he takes the short cuts at work, he's not fond of non-white guys and not shy about telling them. He gets results, and he's secretly a nice guy but don't tell anyone—it'll blow his rep.
4. Jim Rockford from *Rockford Files*. He's legit, sort of. He delivers what the client is looking for. He's not adverse to a woman's charms. He's willing to walk a block to avoid violence. He's got good hair and lives in a trailer—but it's a trailer overlooking the Pacific Ocean. My personal icon.

5. Sargent Joe Friday, *Dragnet*. Just the facts, ma'am. Emotions (and adjectives) are for amateurs.
6. Frasier. He's smarter than you, and yet, amazingly emotionally idiotic. Introduced cappuccino to American television. Classically funny show.
7. Sam Malone from *Cheers*. He peaked at twenty-four. He wasn't aware of it at the time. He's forty-four now. And just starting to figure things out.
8. Homer Simpson. Works in nuclear energy, drinks at the same bar every night, works around Marge, has dreams of incredible grandeur trying to squeeze inside a life of incredible banality.
9. Bob Newhart. No one paused for comedic effect better than Bob.
10. Simon Cowell from *American Idol*. That wasn't very good and I've gotten rich thinking up funny ways to tell you so, directly.

Video Games

(A synopsis of this section for anyone over thirty: Heroes and villains, heroes and villains on steroids, nuclear heroes and villains.[8])

Heart-Rending Personal Anecdote about the Racial Injustice of Video Games

I have a Vietnamese friend named Tien. She is a thirty-five-year-old graduate of USC's Screenwriting Program. In 2004 and 2005, she was in charge of marketing video games at an L.A.-based dot-com, where they decided to create a game based on the Vietnam War. One of the features they invented was "Kill All the Civilians."

Tien, who moved to the U.S. on April 30, 1975, the day of the fall of Saigon, is about as American as they come, but she couldn't believe that a bunch of white guys could sit around in 2005, discussing a feature called "Kill All the Civilians." No one even

---

8. I don't know a lot about video games. I have bad motor skills so playing them makes me feel worse about myself.

seemed to understand when she said they were a bunch of sick racists. They were, they said, creating games that met the needs of that particular market: the more hyperviolent and warlike, the more popular the games are. If that happened to be racist, well, whatever. They weren't trying to hurt anyone's feelings. A month later, after several more complaints, Tien was fired. A lawyer she consulted said she had a mildly compelling discrimination lawsuit—but nothing too serious.

Contrarian White Guy Who Lives in Brooklyn, Is a Dad, Has a Cool Website and Gives a Mean PowerPoint Presentation at Media Festivals.

Steven Johnson is the author of *Everything Bad is Good for You*. I saw him speak at the 2006 Banff World Television Festival. He is a smart guy who probably knows way more about everything in this book than I do, so if you want to put *The White Guy* down and pick up a copy of *Everything Bad is Good for You*, I can live with that.

When people like me tell stories like the one about the game that had a feature called "Kill All the Civilians," Johnson might just counter by saying that's an ill-formed perspective from someone who knows little about video games, which includes most people from my generation, who grew up listening to Sports Play-by-Play White Guy on our transistor radios, not playing video games. Johnson argues that one of the top games played on the Internet is something called *Civilization*, a game that teaches civic society building—not games where kids learn to kill all the civilians.

Here's how the game makers describe *Civilization* on their website (www.civ3.com/legacy.cfm): "An addictive blend of building, exploration, discovery and conquest. Players match wits against some of history's greatest leaders as they strive to build the ultimate civilization to stand the test of time."

Hey! Sounds a lot like the history of Western civilization! (See chapter 10: The White Guy in Human History.)

Eighteen White Guys Who Changed
Popular Culture (for the better)

1. David Geffen. Upside: discovered the Eagles, dated Joni Mitchell, started his own label, sold it for around a billion, came out as gay man, championed Bill Clinton, became Big Hollywood Kahuna, started Dreamworks with Spielberg and Katzenberg, sold it to Paramount Pictures, championed Obama. How's that for a life's work? Downside: still seems angry.

2. Michael Moore. Upside: plaid, flannel-shirt wearing, left-wing documentary filmmaker with a finely honed sense of social injustice whose films *Roger and Me, Bowling for Columbine, Fahrenheit 911* and *Sicko* turned him into a global icon.[9] Downside: fits the facts to fit the story he's trying to tell. Change your shirt, Mike!

3. Ed Sullivan. Upside: former talent manager who hosted a weekly show that introduced the world to the Beatles, Elvis Presley, George Carlin and Richard Pryor. Downside: may have inspired *American Idol*.

4. Don Arden. Upside: Sharon Osbourne's Dad, music impressario and one of the founding fathers of rock and roll. Downside: Passed on managing the Beatles back in the early '60s, because the future of popular music belonged to America.

5. Robert Redford. Upside: movie star, director, American icon. The godfather of the Sundance film movement. Downside: it's hard on everyone when movie stars grow old.

6. Jann Wenner. Upside: publisher of *Rolling Stone* magazine, Wenner was the first person to take the rebellious energy of the 1960s and turn it into a moneymaking enterprise, which people from that generation both love and loathe him for. Downside: four decades worth of highly dubious haircuts.

---

9. Oh! I almost forgot. And the author of *Stupid White Men*, to which this is the spiritual sequel of sorts, minus the conspiracies and partisan furor. I left my partisan furor in my other pants.

7. **Elvis Presley.** Upside: Mississippi white guy blues singer who put the mojo back into music in the 1950s, becoming a global icon known for his excessive lifestyle, weight problems and sequined white jump suits. Downside: to paraphrase Carolyn, my beautiful, elegant, loquacious, sophisticated mother-in-law: he stole that from black people!

8. **John Lennon.** Upside: One quarter of the Beatles, the Liverpool pop group most people consider the greatest band of all time. A peace activist and icon for millions. Downside: why'd you have to die, John?

9. **Billy Wilder.** Upside: German expatriate movie director and probably the greatest screenwriter of all time. Writer and director of such classics as *Sunset Boulevard, The Apartment* and *Some Like It Hot.* Downside: at a studio meeting in the late 1990s, the studio exec, a nice Ivy League grad in his thirties, asks, "Would I know your work?"

10. **Bob Dylan.** Upside: greatest songwriter ever? Downside: worst singer ever. Upside: Being from Minnesota. Downside: *Renaldo and Clara,* Dylan's directorial debut. Four hours of my life I can never get back.

11. **Elmore Leonard.** Upside: Crime novelist and one of the best dialogue writers ever. Downside: stayed in Detroit. Hey Elmore: are you *nuts?* Even poor people leave Detroit because they find it too nasty.

12. **Steven Bochco.** Upside: television producer and creator of *Hill Street Blues* and NYPD *Blue* and writer for *The Rockford Files,* three seminal television dramas that demonstrated you could be funny as well as dramatic on a cop show. Set the stage for *The Sopranos.* Changed the way television was conceived, and made it better. Downside: still a TV writer!

13. **Walt Disney.** Upside: creator of the most influential movie studio of all time. Downside: chain smoker (six packs a day!) and anti-Semite *extraordinaire.*

14. Norman Lear. Upside: television producer and creator of *All in the Family* and a dozen other hit sitcoms. The Steven Bochco of the situation comedy. Changed the way television talked about things like race, class and feminism in the United States in a way that was hilarious. Downside: didn't divorce wife until he sold the syndication rights to all of his shows, costing him about $100 million in the process. Ouch!

15. Steve Jobs. Upside: Invented Apple Computers. Pixar. The iPod. The iPhone. Downside: All those joggers getting peeled off the pavement because they didn't hear the approaching bus.

16. Brad Bird. Upside: director and creator of many children's classics such as *The Iron Giant, The Incredibles* and *Ratatouille*. Downside: all the bad imitators he inadvertently spawned whose movies your kid wants to see, too, because he can't tell the difference between them and a Brad Bird film.

17. George Lucas. Upside: director of *Star Wars* and *American Graffiti* and creator of Lucasfilm Studios in Northern California. Probably the most influential filmmaker of the late-twentieth century. Downside: Probably the most influential filmmaker of the late-twentieth century.

18. George Clooney. Upside: movie star who makes risky, non-commercial movies playing unglamourous anti-heroes except when doing an *Ocean's* sequel. Along with Pitt, Jolie, Damon, Bono and others, uses celebrity as a way of shifting the focus on poverty, disease and high-humidity hotspots around the globe. Downside: "Of my last eight movies, I've only been paid for two," Clooney said at the 2007 Toronto Film Festival. Anti-heroes = anti-paycheque.

We Almost Forgot: The Novel

Whether the novel is a part of popular culture or not is a matter of some confusion. Just take a gander at the daily paper. There's Arts/Entertainment/Lifestyle, and then, once a week, there's that dog-gone Books section, the one whose subtext is Good for You, not

Tastes Great. The *New York Times* has a book section every writer longs to be reviewed in, and also reviews books during the week in its Entertainment section, but then again, New York City is where the bulk of all English books are published, so it figures that there are a lot of people working in industries dedicated to books, a few of whom must read books occasionally.

Elsewhere, not so much.

Novelist White Guy is still around, but he's a bit battered and bruised, much like the medium itself. When he invented the genre, he was British Empire White Guy, way back in the day before there was even an empire. There was just Britain, and for a lot of people, the plumbing sucked, there was no flouride in the water, life was miserable, brutish and short, and all there really was to look forward to was some potato soup for dinner and maybe a pint or ten of ale on payday.

The upside of life then was that the novel was most definitely pop culture. The novel was the primary form of storytelling, along with the theatre. They published novels in newspapers, a new chapter every week, so that Miserable, Toothless, Peasant White Guy could have a few laughs, or a good cry, or just simply an epiphany about life.[10]

One of the first novels ever written was *Robinson Crusoe*, a story about a white guy who goes out on a sailing expedition and ends up shipwrecked on an island filled with non-white guys, where he learns some key lessons about cultural relativism. Although the original title, back in 1719, wasn't *Robinson Crusoe*, it was:

The Life and most Surprizing Adventures of Robinson Crusoe of York, Mariner: who lived Eight and Twenty Years, all alone in an uninhabited Island on the coast of America, lying near the Mouth of

---

10. Unfortunately, the epiphany was that life sucks, you get black lung disease from working in a coal mine, your kids grow up to be drunken, bitter soccer hooligans and the Queen only grows richer.

the Great River of Oroonoque; Having been cast on Shore by Ship-
wreck, wherein all the Men perished but himself. With An Account
how he was at last as strangely deliver'd by Pyrates.

Catchy. (It was a big hit!)

The most popular early Novelist White Guy was Charles Dick-
ens, who wrote about everyone in London back in the day, when
London was quite a bit below average regarding personal hygiene.
As the years went on, White Guy novelist grew in stature. There
was a whole crop of them: E.M. Forster, Thomas Hardy, Joseph
Conrad, Dostoevsky, Flaubert, William James, Tolstoy, Proust,
Hemingway, Norman Mailer, Phil Roth, Saul Bellow, Joseph Hel-
ler and then Martin Amis, Julian Barnes, Martin's pop Kingsley,
along with the odd genius type, like Thomas Pynchon. There was
Günter Grass, the Mann Brothers, Peter Carey, Mordechai Richler
and Robertson Davies and well—it's a long list. For as long as there
has been a printing press, there's been a white guy typing away in
his basement, determined to make the Booker Prize longlist in
order to get invited to better cocktail parties and flirt with prettier,
wittier book publicists called Sam (short for Samantha) or Daisy
(short for Margaret) or Kitty (don't ask).

Well, all you need to know about how things are going for
White Guy Novelist is that it turned out that Günter Grass, author
of *The Tin Drum*, winner of the Nobel Prize for Literature, the man
whose middle name for the past sixty years was "the conscience of
postwar Germany," actually fought for the ss during World War II.
He just didn't bother to tell anyone until 2006! So much for being
the conscience of post-war Germany!

Now it's the twenty-first century. Loads of white guys still write,
but over the past fifty years the novel, much like baseball or basketball, has become a form excelled at more by non-white guys and
even more so, by non-white, non-guys, or simply non-guys.

British Empire White Guy, who was busy with trade routes and
a pitcher of gin in the tropics, didn't count on this: all those years

spent drilling British culture into non-white guys and non-white non-guys resulted in them *becoming* British literary Culture!

Nowadays, some of the best novelists are Zadie (non-white, non-guy) Smith, Rohinton (non-white guy) Mistry, Monica Ali, Kiran Desai and Vikram Seth. There's Michael Ondaatje and Rawi Hage and Jaspreet Singh and M.G. Vassanji and Anosh Irani, who are all, improbably, some of Canada's best writers. There's Salman Rushdie, who was so far ahead of us in predicting the Muslim craziness, I wish he'd been secretary of state. At least he has a clue.

So while it's utterly possible that the novel still is a peripheral part of pop culture, it's also at best, a peripheral part of white guy culture.

And you know what else?

That's okay!

I've been reading a lot of non-white guy, or even non-guy novels lately, and they're great novels. *De Niro's Game* by Rawi Hage. *Such a Long Journey* by Rohinton Mistry. *White Teeth* by Zadie Smith is one of the best novels I've ever read, right up there with *Crime and Punishment, Lonesome Dove, The World According to Garp* and *The Corrections* on my top five. And reading novels by non-white, non-guys or even non-white guys feels interesting. They're windows into worlds I could never otherwise venture into, windows into the collateral fallout of all those empires white guys spent centuries building around the world, now that the empires are collapsing. In *De Niro's Game*, the protagonist, Bassam, grows up in Beirut, a Christian Arab caught in a vicious civil war, studying at a Catholic school run by French Jesuit White Guy. That about sums up the mess the world is in.

(And we still have Houllebeqc! See #4, below.)

Ten Whitest Books of All Time

10. Huckleberry Finn, Mark Twain. Epic adventures of a young white guy and his non-white guy pal back when "America" was still a

dream worth pursuing. Filled with picaresque adventures, down-to-earth racial epithets and a genuine American sense of wonder.

9. **Lonesome Dove**, Larry McMurtry. Two aging Texas Ranger white guys go on one last, long cattle drive late in the nineteenth century. Filled with male bonding, epic man vs. nature conflicts, plenty of non-white guy evil villains, pretty whores and loads of action. Dusty example of Adventure Travel White Guys.

8. **Crime and Punishment**, Fyodor Dostoevsky. A seething student white guy kills the landlady and her daughter, and gets away with it, until his conscience gets the best of him. Tenant fantasy classic whose Detective Porfiry inspired the character of TV's Lieutenant Columbo.

7. **The World According to Garp**, John Irving. A white guy writer's eccentric life of emotionally disengaged, mildly amusing incidents occasionally interrupted by spasms of sex, violence or both. Sort of like the twentieth century.

6. **The Magna Carta.** First draft of the rules of democracy, human rights, etc., etc. Parliamentary democracy, yada, yada, yada. Didn't stop Britain from thinking the rest of the world was its cottage country for the next eight centuries.[11]

5. **Dialogues**, Plato. The earliest philosophy texts, which led to the Magna Carta, which led to the U.S. Constitution, which led to the Bush Dynasty, which led to the liberation of Iraq. Maybe Plato would like a rewrite?

4. **Platform**, Michel Houllebecq. Mildly depressed, emotionally alienated Parisian culture worker dating a tourism operator invents the twenty-first-century version of Adventure Travel White Guy: sexual tourism in the Third World, where First World W people go for holidays and have sex with the attractive, local poor people.

---

11. On September 24, 1215, Pope Innocent III excommunicated all the English lords who had signed the Magna Carta, which he considered a serious challenge to the Catholic Church's authority. Plus ça change.

3. The Corrections, Jonathan Franzen. Middle American white guy writer and his terribly dysfunctional Midwestern family battle to overcome their emotional obstacles amidst a reasonable lifestyle marred only by writer guy son's embarrassing foreign misadventures and sexual harassment lawsuits. And he refused to go on *Oprah!*

2. The Holy Bible. The first draft of Mel Gibson's *The Passion of the Christ*. Needed a rewrite. Too unfocused. Too many characters. Not clear what the conflict is. Too episodic. Apparently Bethlehem is in Occupied Palestine; can we change the location to the (San Fernando) Valley? Pass.

1. The US Constitution. All guys are created equal and deserve life, liberty and the pursuit of happiness. Unless you're a non-white guy or a non-guy. Then all bets are off.

Chapter Summary

The novel was created by a W guy in England, but thanks to four hundred years of plots, W guys have basically run out of storytelling steam, leaving the genre to non-W guys and non-guys, who still have a few excellent stories to tell.

SPORTS

· · ·

GUYS, AS HISTORY shows over and over and over again, do not have a natural affinity for one another. We feel threatened by guys we don't know, and want to kill them, although these days that is generally frowned upon in polite and even impolite, chewing-with-your-mouth-open, drinking-beer-out-of-the-bottle society. Fact is, there is simply a finite amount of anything—homes, jobs, food, women—and way too many guys out there, all thinking the exact same thought:

Scarlett Johansson is *so* hot.

The way we winnow out the weak is to let guys kick the shit out of each other competing for the scraps. That's what's cool about sports.

Sports takes the male's most primitive impulses—as well as a few of our more recently learned ones, such as branding, blogging, smack-talking and product placement—and shoehorns them all into a glorious, televised, competitive spectacle that gets played out in front of tens of millions of fans, who collectively pay hundreds of millions of dollars to witness it. At the end of the day, a lot of athletes, owners and network executives make a wad of money, while millions of hypercompetitive, over-aggressive, emotionally illiterate guys—who, at another moment in history, would be out trying to decapitate one another—bond after the game, sitting in traffic waiting for their turn to vent into their cell phones on the call-in show.

The White Guy has always loved watching sports, even if, these days, that usually means paying mega-bucks to watch non-white guys play the sports we love way better than we can. In fact, millions of white guys seem to love sports more than almost anything—personal grooming, spending time with the fam, having sex, earning a living. Do we need an explanation for this? Maybe, if you're not a sports fan. If you are, it's completely obvious.

Maybe sports is so beloved because it's the White Guy's version of the soap opera, or *telenovela*.[1] Our emotional lives get played out through the dramas of our favourite athletes, their wins, losses, triumphs, heartbreaks and of course, their nine-figure contracts and palatial home purchases, which we will never enjoy ourselves, all in a way that's totally masculine and not suspect, like having season tickets to the opera or joining a men's group. For what is a night at almost any bar anywhere in the world, the night the local heroes are playing on TV, but one, big socially acceptable men's group, minus the drums and awful, over-earnest poetry? There's bonding, there's sharing, and yes, there's apt to be hugging aplenty at the end of the night, if all goes well.

Maybe even a bum slap or two if it was a division rival your guys defeated.

Of course, considering that non-white guys are most often the athletes and white guys are the paying customers and the media who report on the athletes, there is loads of racial subtext in sports,

---

1. That's what they call those Mexican soap operas you occasionally stumble across when you punch in Univision while trying to find *SportsCenter*.

much of it nasty, which is unfortunate. Sometimes it's a lot worse than unfortunate, but we are not talking about polite society here; we are talking about guys, beer, wins, beer, losses, beer, oh and how about another round of beer? The fact is that there are many, many teams, and very few champions. There are also many, many columnists, talk shows and bloggers, many dedicated to finding someone to blame when things don't go so well, and guess who frequently finds themselves feeling the heat of defeat?

Anyone who ever followed the trail of tears left by football stars Terrell Owens and Michael Vick or the winsome ways of Barry Bonds, the home run king, knows what I'm talking about. Sports has become a multibillion dollar dance, with the non-white guys playing and the white guys paying, talking and writing about them.

Sports White Guys Who Needed to Get a Rewrite

1. Jimmy the Greek, former CBS football broadcaster. Said in 1988 that blacks make the best athletes because they were bred as slaves to be big. He also said white guys keep all the management and broadcasting jobs for themselves because that's all that's left for them in sports.
2. Al Campanis, ex-L.A. Dodgers GM. Said blacks weren't mentally fit for management positions.
3. John Rocker, former Atlanta Braves' closer. Hated all those who ride the 7 train to Shea Stadium in New York: "Some kid with purple hair, next to some *queer* with AIDS, right next to some dude who just got out of jail for the fourth time, right next to some twenty-year-old mom with four kids . . ."
4. Don Imus, WFAN shock jock. Described some Rutgers' women's basketball players as "nappy-headed 'hos"—and he said much worse over forty years on the radio.
5. Howard Cosell, former *Monday Night Football* icon. Grew up idolizing Jackie Robinson, was Willie May's lawyer and supported Muhammad Ali's refusal to fight in Vietnam, but in

1983 referred, on air, to Washington Redskin's non-white guy wide receiver Alvin Garrett as a "little monkey." It's a generational thing.

WHILE SOME PEOPLE find the sort of racial bickering that sports is loaded with disturbing, or juvenile, or a sign of a culture that is still deeply racially polarized, at least sports fans talk about it. Sports gets to the racial conversation well ahead of the rest of the culture.

It has to. Sports is integrated. At least it has been, since Jackie Robinson in 1947 (a mere thirty-seven years before MTV was still not playing non-white guy Michael Jackson's videos before his record label threatened to go medieval on them).

Look what's happened to baseball since Jackie got everyone used to having a non-white guy in the lineup. First it was African-Americans. Then it was Central Americans. Then, Canadians and Asians.

As Melanee says, the good thing about sports that has always benefitted the non-white guy is that it's not subjective, in a way. If you can outperform everyone else, it's pretty self-apparent, something that was never demonstrated more clearly than in 1965, when Texas El-Paso beat the legendary University of Kentucky team (coached by Adolph Rupp) dressing five non-white guy starters, the first time that had ever happened in NCAA history.

Even the average NHL dressing room these days is full of different languages: French, English, Swedish, Russian. The San Antonio Spurs, the greatest NBA franchise of the past ten years, with four world titles to its name, has a dozen key players, including a French non-white guy (married to a Latina television star), two Argentines, a defensive specialist and a boring, methodical, utterly reliable, unselfish genius from the Virgin Islands named Tim Duncan, all coached by a pockmarked ex-Marine white guy named Popovich. The Spurs are the freaking UN, only they all have to get on the plane together and find a way to get along. Despite all sorts of cultural landmines, and the mega-egos of professional athletes, they do (although the over-under on Tony Parker and Eva Longoria's marriage is still thirty months).

Of course, nowadays, what makes white guys angry isn't the presence of non-white guys playing games better than they ever could. It's the money.

They make so much money. And so many of them have such bad attitudes. And tickets cost so much. It's just such a turnoff.

Well, for all of you angry white guys who feel you've been pushed aside, remember: there are *still* sports white guys excel at, including pro hockey, auto racing, poker playing, professional rodeo, downhill skiing, ultimate fighting, competitive surfing, golf, tennis, extreme sports, bass fishing, luge and spelling bees.

The great thing about many of these sports is that they require either a) money, b) winter or c) nature, three things non-white guys around the world have historically had much less access to.[2]

And look at the upside. In 2010, South Africa will host the World Cup of Soccer, the biggest TV event in the world. Twenty years ago, South Africa was still run by white guys trying to convince the world that Apartheid was a legitimate way to run a country. Now the game that was developed by British Empire White Guy between bowls of inedible gruel at the boarding school has become one of the ways in which the whole world finds reasons to stop their fighting and commune in front of the TV.

In the summer of 2007, Iraq stopped blowing itself to bits to watch its national soccer team beat Saudi Arabia and win the Asian Cup soccer championship. It was the first time in four years that the bullets were flying out of celebration, aimed at no one but the sky.

In Liberia, international soccer star George Weah, the 1995 FIFA World Player of the Year, returned home from Europe and the U.S., where he earned millions of dollars, to run for president.

---

2. Also a nice pot connection helps if you plan to pursue a career doing triple flips off a ramp on a skateboard.

He lost—but his candidacy galvanized the lost boys there, who had traded in their education and childhoods to pick up guns and fight a war. Weah caused them to put down their guns and get politicized and try to build their country another way.

All of which is sort of amazing, when you stop and think about it. Sports often achieves what all the politicians and states and armies and diplomats try to achieve, and simply flounder at: it finds reasons for guys to put down their guns and hoist a beer together.

Ten Sports White Guys Still Play Better Than Almost Anyone, If You Don't Count Tiger Woods and Jarome Iginla

1. NASCAR. Leadfoots turning left all day and cursing at the other drivers—or worse. Sounds like most of our lives.
2. Hockey. A lot of toothless white guys from places like Kirkland Lake and Slovenia and Malmo wearing thirty pounds of protective equipment, firing hard rubber at a hundred miles an hour and fighting by pulling the other guy's sweater over his head. I love this game!
3. Tennis. A lot of white guys from the Nick Bollettieri Tennis Academy trying to find a weakness in the impenetrable game of Roger Federer, the greatest athlete in history to have a fairly chunky, ordinary looking fiancée. Maybe Roger knows something Tiger doesn't.
4. Golf. Tiger Woods and Vijay Singh excluded, no sport was ever devised that better exploits the limited emotional life of white guys. Golf is a sport that must be executed with mathematical precision, all while attempting to suppress your emotions even though you are dressed like it's the Mardi Gras Parade.
5. Luge. White guys dressed like sperm barrel down icy chutes once every four years.
6. Pro rodeo. Anyone up for a night at the chuck wagon races?
7. Bass Fishing. White guys in boats paddling around a lake, trying to catch supper—and about 100K.

8. Snowboard cross. Twentysomething white guys fresh from the X Games boarding down some serious moguls.
9. Ultimate fighting. You know that movie where the nerdy accountant guy discovers working out and turns into a warrior? Meet Chuck Liddell, the toughest two hundred pounds of white guy this side of Chris Pronger.
10. Horseracing. Five-foot-tall white guys who weigh 112 pounds, living one peanut at a time.

Chapter Summary

Sports occupy a dominant spot in the recreational life of the White Guy, although these days we are not very good at the most popular ones.

THE PURSUIT OF EXCELLENCE VS.
THE NEW MEDIOCRITY

PREHISTORIC ERA WHITE GUY pursued dinner. Depression Era White Guy pursued work. Hippie Era White Guy pursued peace and love. New Millenium White Guy pursued undervalued startups. Every era throughout history has featured a bunch of white guys pursuing something, but as the eras unwind, the urgency to pursue life's essentials has dwindled, leaving a whole segment of the population—the wealthiest, healthiest, best-educated, best-connected white guys—to concentrate on pursuing one thing: exclusive, unvarnished, relentless *excellence*.

Excellence isn't always easy to recognize, although luckily for the people who pursue it, it often comes accompanied by substantial budgets for advertising that doesn't beat around the bush about what it's selling. (If you doubt me, leaf through a copy of *Vanity Fair*.)

The Pursuit of Excellence has driven the privileged W People of the planet for centuries now. These days it has become increasingly democratized, producing a lot of less-privileged, super-anxious white guys who are terrified of falling into the abyss so many white guys seem to land in, particularly if they're dads: the abyss of mediocrity.

If you want to scare the bejesus out of a twenty-two-year-old white guy with high hopes for life, just whisper the "m" word into his ear and watch him turn a whiter shade of pale. Sure, Baghdad is dodgy the moment you walk outside the Green Zone; sailing solo across the North Atlantic is scary, and ice climbing with no rope up the face of a mountain in Central Asia can get the heart racing; but all of it sounds better than a life spent being unremarkably, predictably, relentlessly *average*.

Or does it? Maybe mediocrity is just the wrong word for the right way to live your life. Maybe—work with me here—the only thing misguided about mediocrity is that it lacks the advertising budget that Excellence has always enjoyed.

Maybe all mediocrity needs is a makeover!

EXCELLENCE IS SOMETHING the white guy frequently finds himself hotly in pursuit of. Excellence is what separates the truly unique individual from the seething masses, particularly if he has a credit score over seven hundred and no kids to schlep to soccer.

Excellence is what happens when someone dedicates himself to a goal, rather than being swept through life by the conventional wisdom of the day, the one that dictates your brand of jeans, the size of your cell phone or where you go for drinks with all your friends.

Excellent is how fulfilled people feel.

There are excellent restaurants, novels, cities, vacation spots, scotch and—*bien sûr*—*fromage!* There is a whole culture dedicated to pursuing what's excellent and leaving the mundane behind.

If you have to ask where, never you mind.

Some days, so much excellence beckons that it's difficult to get out of bed, knowing as you do that so much of your life will be given over to the pursuit of something quite a bit less than excellent.

Hello mediocrity, my old friend.

MEDIOCRITY COMES IN many forms, but probably no single place hollers "mediocre" quite so relentlessly as Canada. Aside from Canada's spectacular natural beauty and wealth of natural resources, the country seems constitutionally mandated to observe a collective mediocrity, a need for no one to rise above anyone else, a seething reasonableness, an overwhelming urge to make the sensible choice.

Canada is a country that won't go to war with anyone unless the United Nations is on board with the idea. Even then, we are far more comfortable playing the peacekeepers, the blue hats, the referees willing to stand between the combatants in order for sanity to prevail. That's why we're Canada. We're so damn... willing to adhere to international organizations.

Then there's Canadian people.

Aside from the odd serial killer, corporate criminal Bernie Ebbers, or Vegas icon Céline Dion, Canadians are raised from childhood to be, above all else, reasonable. We try to see both sides of every argument. We don't shove our cultural values down your throat.

However, it is becoming almost disturbingly apparent that there are a few things Canadians excel at, which makes a country that brags about its bronze medals *anxious*.

For example, Canadians excel in journalism, which seeks the objective point of view (as opposed to American journalists, who find it helps to burst into tears on camera); comedy, a kind of emotional detachment from the world; female singer-songwriters, who bare their souls in verse, over some quite middling acoustic guitar-playing; and hockey, a speedy, violent game that allows you to kick the crap out of your opponents when the occasion calls for it—and when you lose in the playoffs, you line up and shake the hands of the guys who kicked the crap out of you.

Then there's that Blackberry guy, Jim Balsillie: multibillionaire, would-be NHL owner, sponsor of internationalist forums who still drives his kids to school every morning. If only he had hair, he'd be perfect.

The Canadian economy is strong. The Canadian government practices fiscal responsibility. Canada features universal healthcare, although most Canadians would argue that it is universally inept. Canadian universities charge reasonable tuition and offer a generally high level of academic instruction. (We won't talk about how Canada mangles the environment.)

If Canada isn't careful, it might start giving mediocrity a good name.

I appreciate excellence. Once in a while, I stumble upon it. If I happen to eat somewhere excellent, I count myself lucky. If the game I'm watching—e.g., the 2008 NFC Division Final between the Giants and the Packers—turns out to be excellent, that's pretty much like finding money on the sidewalk.

I grew up in Winnipeg, where pursuing excellence is considered anti-social, deviant behavior. In Winnipeg, the worst thing a person could be was "too into himself." In the U.S., this is called being "focused."

The white guy's terror of mediocrity might have something to do with British Empire White Guy, at least Upper Class Twit British Empire White Guy, who has never been shy about ripping mediocrity as the worst sort of character flaw, as if mediocrity-worship is the reason why The Country Formerly Known as an Empire is now down to one lousy island, some amusing television chefs and a lot of Russian oligarchs living in Belgravian mansions that cost a bloody fortune to heat.

Pursuit of Excellence White Guy (PoEWG) is careful about making a commitment to anything—a person, a job, a living space or an automobile—lest it prove to be anything less than excellent.

PoEWGs like (young) Warren Beatty take years between film projects. They control every aspect of production. They do things over and over and over again until they're perfect. Filming the climactic death scene in *McCabe and Mrs. Miller* in British Columbia in 1972, Beatty died a couple times for director Robert Altman, who was notorious for his preference for improvisation and didn't believe in shooting one take after another, because that sucked the life out of a scene.

After a few takes, Altman was happy. It was 7:30 at night. It was winter. It was time to go for a drink.

"That's a wrap," Altman goes.

Whereupon Beatty goes, "Bob, I think there's a few other ways I can die in this scene. We just did three or four takes."

"It doesn't get better after three or four takes, Warren," Altman says. "I like it spontaneous."

"I think there are a lot of ways to explore death," Beatty says.

That's when Altman stands.

"Fine, Warren," Altman goes. "You do as many takes of the scene as you like. I'm going for a drink." Or seven. And then, Altman walks off the set—of his own movie.

Instead of being embarrassed about being a high-maintenance, whining control freak, Beatty keeps the crew on the set and shoots his death scene sixty more times, until he gets it absolutely perfect.[1]

Recently I met a Canadian academic writing a PhD thesis about the ethics of mediocrity.[2] According to him, Ancient Greek White Guy thought mediocrity was something to which a person should *aspire*, not something one should be ashamed of, like having body odour, loving the Chicago Cubs or reading crime novels.

It wasn't until the Romans showed up that mediocrity got a bad name. The world wouldn't see a crew as debauched and excessive as the Romans until Keith Richards met Marianne Faithful—and they shot each other full of heroin. The Romans sacrificed people to the lions for sport. They ate and drank until they vomited, then they ate and drank some more. They took over the world, then made the world wear those dopey plumed helmets and frat-house

---

1. This anecdote courtesy of Peter Biskind's *Easy Riders, Raging Bulls,* Simon & Schuster, 1998.

2. What a perfect topic for a Canadian academic, I told him. He didn't find that funny.

togas and open-toed sandals and grapes in their hair. They tossed
unwanted Christian babies on a pile outside of town. Oh yeah. And
they killed Jesus.

Did I mention the orgies?

What was this, an entire culture acting like it was the '70s and
they were trying to get into Studio 54?

These are the people who sold the idea that mediocrity is something to be ashamed of?

PoEWG SEES A LOT of the guys he went to school with sliding into
the Abyss of the Ordinary, and it scares the heck out of him.

The greatest writer ever to live on the Upper East Side was Harold Brodkey. He wrote legendary short stories in the late 1950s that
smart Manhattan people all talked about. He was tall and charis-
matic, smart and funny, and great at dinner parties. He was Harold
freaking Brodkey! In 1964 he got an advance to write a great novel
for Random House. It was expected that he'd be finished his great
novel in about eighteen months.

In 1976 he turned in a manuscript that was rumoured to
be two thousand pages long.

In 1991 the novel, *The Runaway Soul*, was published. No one
cared.

New Mediocrity White Guy (NMWG), who once was Minimalist,
Austere, Beatnik-Hobo White Guy, whose entire life fit into a sin-
gle bag, who hand-wrote long, ironic poems about the joys of going
Greyhound, who hitchhiked, understands it's not the '70s anymore.

Sometimes, you just need to own stuff, stuff that has to fit in
the car or else the kid will simply start *howling*.

PoEWG can be found anywhere,[3] discovering places no white
guy has visited before (highly difficult), restaurants no one knows

---

3. Anywhere excellence is pursued, that is. That eliminates the Midwest, Florida—
apart from South Beach—and Belgium, although they do have a talent with
chocolate. And Canada.

about (ha!) or new ways to have the most excellent orgasm ever. PoEWG frequently moves to New York, to escape the mediocrity that dominates everywhere else.

NMWG doesn't need a GPS in the car. NMWG would just as soon attach the stroller to his bike and cycle somewhere.

PoEWG downloads all the hottest new songs. He's into alternative/positive hip hop/world beat/new pop. Also likes a lot of old Elton John songs—but don't tell anyone.

NMWG can live with the fact that his kid likes to hide his John Mellencamp CDs in all the places a two-foot-tall kid can hide a CD.

In New York, he works until 8 PM, spends 65 percent of his income on an embarrassingly bad apartment, then spends whatever time he has left waiting to get seated at any restaurant that will seat him, because he's so hungry he's going to cry.

PoEWG only goes to see excellent foreign and indie films, but those don't stick around too long these days.

Can you say "another Netflix Saturday night"?

NMWG loves Pixar movies. Gone are Francis Ford Coppola movies, Bobby De Niro movies, Marty Scorsese movies—and that's okay. (He did sneak out to the mall to see *The Departed*, which was good, but not great. Not Marty Scorcese great. It was Marty's New Mediocrity Classic!)

PoEWG goes to excellent clubs, but isn't as young as he used to be.

NMWG never gets out to see a new band. Unless it's a lunchtime concert, close to work.

PoEWG doesn't eat lunch. Lunch is for mediocre people. PoEWG uses lunch to train for triathalons.

The New Mediocrity is already happening. There's a whole new generation of Slacker Dads, guys in their twenties and thirties who woke up, looked around, saw a world where the divorce rate is through the roof—often including their own parents—and just said, oh, screw it. Think I'll have a kid and stick around to raise it. It will involve sleep deprivation, early nights, lots of walks around the neighbourhood, lots of hours at the playground and trading in

The Sopranos for *That's So Raven*. It will never pay off financially. The sex will suffer. There will never be quite enough time alone to create anything truly great; that's for solitary geniuses.

Anyone for a humour book with lots of ironic illustrations, chapter summaries, cute talk-show-like lists and enough Canadian content for the publisher to get his grant next year?

The poster child for the New Mediocrity would have to be Ron Howard, the movie director. Nice guy, even though he was a child star. Lost his hair young, a catastrophe for an actor. Switched to director and now he runs Imagine Entertainment, and won an Oscar, making films that tend not to push the envelope anywhere. Stayed married.

POEWG eventually does what everyone in New York does: gets into real estate, come hell or high water. If Leonardo da Vinci was still alive, he would have found a way to rustle up the down payment for a condo on East 2nd Street. It's the only way. In the meantime, the city is safer than ever. There's kids everywhere. Hey! Who let all these loud, self-absorbed, spoiled, noisy brats into New York City? Don't they get it? It's New York freaking City! Excellence: yes. Kids: no!

NMWG doesn't even have a full-time job. He's one of those tele-commuting web content providers who works out of the café on the corner, emailing content to some far-flung corner of the world while the kid snoozes next to him in the stroller because there's nowhere to work at home in the rent-controlled one-bedroom apartment with the view of the fire escape next door. Brother, can you spare a low-APR credit card for six months? My interest payments have got me down.

POEWG only dates women between eighteen and twenty-three. After that, they're too into getting serious. Seriousness is not excellent if you're POEWG. He has too many personal goals to achieve to be in a relationship, one of which is to sleep with as many women as possible.

NMWG splits the day up with his wife so she can pursue her goals too.

POEWG thinks there is no higher form of sanity than living in the present moment. He learned that from reading Pat Riley's autobiography. He learned a lot from Pat Riley.

POEWG reads the *New York Times*, the *New York Observer*, the *Guardian Weekly*, *Daily Variety*, the *Economist* and the *Globe and Mail*.

NMWG gets a kick out of Page 6. He can read *Vanity Fair* without seething that he's not in it. Tom Cruise and Katie Holmes' kid is actually quite cute.

POEWG is in *Vanity Fair*. He specifically asked not to be in an issue featuring celebrity baby photos, although he would make an exception for Brad and Angie, who are really sweet, in addition to being so committed to social change.

In a way, Buddhism is a kind of mediocrity-based religion. It's about balance. No one points out that balance is the opposite of Roman Catholicism, which is sort of hardcore about how it expects Roman Catholic people to behave.

POEWG is into maximizing personal potential.

In a way, dads are the Buddhists of white guys. They're plunged into mediocrity, and expected to love it, in a media universe toasting the pursuit of excellence—but what else would the media universe toast, given that all those hyper-expensive products buying ads in magazines are the ones driving the editorial message? There aren't too many ads in *Vanity Fair* about getting the sensible, generic four-door sedan with airbags. Because God knows we all need a Porsche Carrera with no back seat that will do 180 mph around sharp turns. That'll get the kid to his sleep-over on time.

POEWG only wears the best, sleeps between sheets with the highest thread count ever recorded, drinks zero malt scotch flown overnight from a bog in the Scottish Highlands, eats the rawest food known to man and stays in suites at the Four Seasons.

Someday, he'll meet that certain someone. Until then, $1,500 a night hookers will have to do.

Sometimes, the most excellent thing in the world is when Dad comes through the door after work.

Ten Cases of the Misguided Pursuit of Excellence

10. Exploring outer space. It's out there, you can't breathe, you float instead of walking, there's nothing but rock and leftover space shuttle parts and it's millions of years to the next solar system. Now build some goddamn levees with those billions you'll save not going into space!

9. Excellent golf gear. It's not quite Scientology, but is there anything more boring than a table full of white guys dressed in golf leisure wear talking about their gear? And I love golf! I just feel as if I've stumbled upon a well-fed, married version of those glassy-eyed, Hari Krishnas who dress in orange and do the odd set on the Third Street Promenade every weekend in Santa Monica.

8. Perfecting yourself. If we wanted people to be perfect, we'd get Steve Young, the handsome, articulate former quarterback of the 49ers who has a law degree, to be the dad of *everyone*.

7. Totally original bands. Who hate to say who their influences are. There are no totally original bands, and if there are, you better search under the bed for their Unabomber Manifesto.

6. The perfect Pinot Noir. I know, I know—I'm one of the people who thought *Sideways* deserved the hype. But people, please! Every time I go into my local upscale, intimate wine store, I am paralyzed by adjectives plastered everywhere (fruity, fragrant, piquant, cassis). Just pour me a glass of plonk, for chrissakes!

5. Excellent women. Jared Paul Stern, former *New York Post* gossip monger, once said, "Every time you see a beautiful woman, just remember that somewhere, there's a guy who's totally sick of her." Maybe it's time to grow up and advance to the next stage, the one after She's Totally Hot, Dude!

4. Excellent investments. If they're so excellent, why is this guy you've never met telling you about it in an email that landed in "junk"?

3. The perfect parent. Trying to be perfect on that little sleep is a recipe for self-immolation.

2. The perfect hotel. The fancier the hotel, the more I get the heebie-jeebies in the room that as soon as I leave, the entire place will be dusted for fingerprints and I will be dinged six or seven hundred bucks in surprise charges.

1. The perfect life. If nothing ever went wrong, or broke your heart, or you never got sick, you wouldn't ever be able to appreciate when things go well.

Ten Habits of the New Mediocrity

10. Early to bed. Nothing good ever happens after midnight, or so I'm told.

9. Lovely leftovers. Someone needs to make an Ang Lee–style food movie about turning whatever's left in the fridge into dinner.

8. One more year. The saga of trying to get your beater, with exactly 131,100 miles on it, to pass the California smog test, every other year, well into the twenty-first century.

7. Room with a view (of the building next door). An E.M. Forster–esque romance about living eight years in a one-bedroom, rent-controlled apartment in Santa Monica with a young son because you can't afford the cost of California real estate.

6. Quickies. Because that kid is gonna wake up any minute!

5. The children's cinema of the earliest twenty-first century, or, if I see one more digitally animated movie with sarcastic talking animals/insects/sea life/fairy tale characters, I'm going to shoot myself. It's all about the child.

4. Romantic comedies about the middle of relationships. Best exemplified by *Eternal Sunshine of the Spotless Mind*, a film from a Charlie Kaufman script that explores the part of the relationship

where you really aren't that into the other person but can't live
without them.

3. Catchy songs that are upbeat about life. F— off and die.

2. Lists! And books that are full of them.

1. Upbeat punctuation. If we want to be upbeat, we'll be upbeat.
Writers who rely upon excessively emotional punctuation are
like wine stores who rely upon excessive adjectives to justify their
excessive prices. Shove that exclamation mark back into the dark
hole with all your other idiotic emoticons, you typographic loser.
Not that I'm feeling defensive about my exclamation mark habit
or anything.

Interlude Summary

*Inside every white guy there is a wrestling match going on between
his desire to pursue excellence and the mediocrity that usually results.
Wrestling, as you may or may not know, is fake. Mediocrity wins.*

THE WHITE GUY
IN HUMAN HISTORY

. . .

HUMAN HISTORY IS a vast, all-encompassing subject that barely fits into a seven-volume set of
single-spaced history books by people way smarter than I am, let
alone a single chapter of a trade paperback, but that's no reason
not to offer a condensed version of it. Who's got time for seven
volumes?

The way I see it, history is less an unfolding saga of progres-
sive change than a series of recurring themes repeated over and
over again with bigger and stronger guns, ever higher temperatures,
a rising water table and different but ultimately recognizable versions of the same sort of protagonist: a white guy who wants what
you've got, and if you don't give it to him, he'll kill you.

Ever since we first climbed out of a cave all those thousands of
years ago, white guys have prowled the world looking for gold, the
choicest real estate, freedom from the old country and billions in
oil revenue. Along the way, we force fed all the non-white guys we

came across a god, made up some theories that made it okay to keep the best land for ourselves, created countries when ever and wherever it suited the needs of our companies and even thought up reasons why it was okay to own the locals and get them to work free for hundreds of years.

At least that's my understanding of history, and I have a university degree!

Eras, in Brief

He might have been a Greek, boring you to death with his chatter about democratic ideals, until you woke up in time to score tickets to the nude Olympics.

He might have been a Roman, looking for some dinner for his lion.

He might have been a Hun, the earliest version of the 'roid-enraged NFL middle linebacker, out scouring mountain villages for hidden riches and virgins.

He might have been a European king, spinning the idea that God made him do it.

He might have been Olga the Viking, who invaded England, provoking all those pub-crawling, poetry-writing, non-teeth brushing, duel-loving Saxon heathens to convert to Christianity, which for a minute made it look as if the eleventh century really was going to belong to the Vikings (sort of the same way the Super Bowl in the 1970s looked as if *it* would belong to the Vikings—until they played the games).

Then, in the eleventh century, not content with England and Scandinavia—would you be?—the Vikings invaded the Greek Empire. Big mistake. Greeks don't play when it comes to home(land) invasions. They devised a flaming coconut bomb (later featured in the film *Swiss Family Robinson*) that set the Vikings' wooden ships on fire, thus bringing to a close their pursuit of global domination. This setback didn't stop other white guys, over and over again for the ensuing thousand years, from taking a crack at the planet.

He might have been a Knight of the Templar in 1100, sacking Jerusalem of all the non-white guys so Christian Guy could run it for a few hundred years.[1]

He might have been Crusades White Guy early in the thirteenth century, seeking out non-Christian Guy anywhere he could find him and breaking the bad news that it was time to convert, and not just from pounds to euros.

The guy could be a pope, with God on his side and the Devil waiting in the wings if you didn't believe him—and just ask all the Mayans and other pagans the Spanish got to if the pope was bluffing.

The guy could be Dutch White Guy, discovering the view off the southern cliffs of Africa and deciding he was staying, he was in charge, end of conversation—until 1994.

He could be British White Guy, deciding that the rest of the world—places like India and Canada and Australia and Hong Kong and Egypt and lots of other countries in Africa and Iraq (!)—would be run better by guys like him. (It was for their own good.)

He could be French White Guy around 1789, who decided, off with the Queen's head, and Sofia Coppola's too for making that nutty movie about Marie Antoinette! Or German White Guy who decided that what the world really needed was no Jews—and body-hugging leather officer's gear. Or he could have been American White Guy, who decided that his strongman had to be in control, whether the citizens of Chile, El Salvador, Guatemala, Vietnam, Iran and Iraq liked it or not.

Along the way, some cool things like the telephone, Major League Baseball, sushi, the flop wedge and the printing press were invented, so that each conflict was a little different than the last.[2]

---

1. According to novelist Jack Whyte, author of *Knights of the Black and White*, the Knights of the Templar were the first soldiers who were authorized to kill in the name of God. I guess it seemed like a good idea at the time.
2. Not all invented by the white guy. We can't take credit for sushi.

However, once you cut out the progress, human history is a shorter chapter than you think.

Ten Worst White Guy Ideas in Human History

1. Everyone must be Christian. This resulted in centuries of bloody conflict, religious wars, genocides and many, many centuries worth of over-the-top passion plays (not to be confused with the films of Zalman King).

2. School is where we teach you how to be white. Canada and Australia both employed the residential school system, which taught Aboriginals not to be Aboriginals. And they say Canadian W People are the nice ones.

3. Let's make every house beige. What would have become of Mr. Benetton's sweater business if this were true?

4. No one owns Africa. All this continent really needs is a little British organization, a little Dutch discipline and a little French style to make it work. Oh, and slaves.

5. Aboriginals don't believe anyone owns the land but white people do so it's ours now. No one forced them to be animistic pagans.

6. I think it works best with a happy ending. That would be the ending where the W people get what they came for, and keep it. Forever.

7. Let the market decide. The market decided it loves rich people.

8. Let's kill all the Jews, AKA, the Holocaust. No one likes them anyways, and they own all the best paintings.

9. We're the civilized ones, and you're the savages. That's why these cluster bombs we're about to drop on you are for your own good. It's just an unfortunate coincidence that kids pick them up because they're painted yellow and look like toys.

10. Everyone is entitled to his political beliefs as long as they agree with ours. Otherwise known as the doctrine of pre-emptive liberation. (This could be subtitled, "*[fill in resource-rich, impoverished, corrupt, chaotic, non-white guy–dominated country here] Only Responds to a Strongman.*"]

Chapter Summary

Since Jesus died, the world has had a problem named "White Guy."

· · · · · · · · · · · · · ·

MEL'S DEEP THOUGHT

(Another in an occasional series of interruptions to the narrative flow)

No. 4: FIRST HUMANS

· · ·

THE COOL thing about Canadian White Guys is that, after beating down their enemy, they hand out lovely consolation prizes. As a result, the indigenous populations of Canada have gone through many name changes over the years, from Indians to Native Americans to Aboriginals to First Nations. Each refinement is a kind of cultural confession, a way for Canadian Ws to acknowledge that they weren't always a bunch of sensible-shoe wearing, liberal good listeners—that in fact, back in the day, some extremely not-so-savoury shenanigans went down between them and the First Nations people, the aftereffects of which are still with us today.

Describing a group as a First Nation also gives some respect to the fact that they were once the sort of force white guys can really relate to: a big, shiny corporation called a nation. In the same spirit, I would like to give African Americans another name change, too.

I consider the naming of black identity to be a decades-old poem, and the effort to find the right word a crucial exercise in the creative process of discovering our true identity. After all, black folks have been through more name changes than just about anyone on the planet. We started out as *niggers*, a white trash rendition of the Spanish word *negre*, which we eventually embraced as *negro* (Spanish sounds so much more romantic than English, don't it?). Then we became *coloured* (why didn't white people become non-coloured?) and then *Afro American*, which got all tangled up in a hairstyle (pun intended) so that it didn't seem quite right.

Nowadays, we interchange *black* with *African American*.
I actually like both terms, and often switch them up (just like I do
with my hair-dos, yaw). Both work for me, without diminishing me
in the eyes of W people and all the others. Both sound all right.

However, it's time for a name change. Which is why I proudly
introduce another refinement in our understanding of just who
black folks actually are...

A certain truth about black people all over the diaspora
needs to be made explicit. No matter how many ancient, DNA-
laden fossils of old African mothers abound, white folks (and
everybody else) seem to be totally amnesiac about the fact that
everybody—and I mean everybody—comes from Africa. Even
Anderson Cooper was shocked to learn about the East African
tribe with whom he shares his DNA (I wonder if he cried).

Why is this astonishment so prevalent in our scientific, anti-
intelligent design world? It's the name, stupid.

So, in addition to being called black and African American,
we will also heretofore be known as First Humans. If that's
not enough to get some casino licenses and free college tuition,
I don't know what is.

And if the ozone layer keeps disappearing and ultra-violet
rays keep on zapping us, we will probably be the last. Humans,
that is.

End of Deep Thought.

. . . .

POLITICAL SYSTEMS

— *or* —

NOTES ON OUR THREE-THOUSAND-YEAR
WINNING STREAK

• • •

*As the twentieth century ended, there were around 120 democracies
in the world—and I can assure you more are on the way.*

PRESIDENT GEORGE W. BUSH, speaking to the
National Endowment for Democracy, November 2003

The Doctrine of Whatever Works

THE WHITE GUY is fond of democracy, but willing
to settle for quite a bit less if that's what's necessary to keep the oil flowing and the companies owned by white
guys everywhere churning out the things companies churn out.
It's all fine and good to claim that we invented democracy, but we
didn't much shy away from our share of absolute monarchies, military dictatorships and racist regimes for the first twenty centuries of
the post-Jesus world, either. A better way to describe the political
preferences of the White Guy might be to say, Whatever Works.

In other words, if you can promise us we'll keep winning, we're for it!

Negative White Guy

While the negatively inclined intellectual such as Naomi Klein might argue that this ultra-pragmatic approach to organizing humanity leaves the door wide open for huge chunks of human misery, much of which, according to her new book *The Shock Doctrine*, is hugely profitable for multi-nationals, I would have to say this is a severe case of viewing this particular glass as half empty.

After all, where would Naomi—as well as her left-wing husband Avi and his do-gooder dad Stephen, who has had a long career of being concerned about the human cost of things—*be* if a long list of white guys who were more concerned with nation building than the human cost of anything hadn't followed a political belief system of Whatever Works?

Does she *honestly* believe she would have been able to earn a nice living and enjoy a nice, cushy Toronto intellectual's lifestyle if some white guy, somewhere, wasn't shouting into a phone to some Third World dictator, saying he doesn't give a damn about refugees, just as long as the Natives don't storm the oil wells? I think *not!*

Yet for every white guy out there finding a way to make a living and build a better grass hut in some high-humidity part of the world where you can barely drink a glass of water without thinking it's your last, there's a negative white guy in some shabby professor's office somewhere, explaining how it's just another example of colonial behaviour. Negative White Guy is a poorer, shabbier-dressed, frustrated version of Bay Area White Guy (see page 182), who is the king of being against shit, but also wealthy, plugged-in, in shape and not stuck in some windowless office somewhere, plotting how to gaslight the chairman of the department.

Political Systems, or White Guys' Greatest Hits, Vol. 1

Here is a short survey of different political systems white guys have embraced over the past twenty centuries.

1. Democracy (The Theory)

Aristotle and Plato thought this was a great theory, although their version of democracy was basically: white guys voting for white guys, while women and non-white guys could just embrace their own political system as soon as they broke free of those shackles that bound them.

2. Democracy (In Practice)

This is much, much messier. In practice, democracy is largely dedicated to trade routes. A thriving democracy requires sturdy institutions, which are apolitical and keep the politicized institutions in check. Something like the Supreme Court Justices, who in 2000 stepped into an electoral fray and handed the election to the Republican candidate. Oh, never mind.

Democracy (In Practice) needs institutions to protect the rights of its least powerful, because why else does the state exist except to ensure that the least powerful citizens aren't trampled by the powerful and wealthy looking to enhance their trade routes? This is known as Congress. Oh, forget it.

Above all, Democracy (In Practice) needs *practice*. Countries can't just wake up and be democratic. It isn't done that way. It's like working out. You don't just wake up with six-pack abs. You need to train. You need to exercise, day after day after day. You need to eat properly, lots of grilled chicken breast and less beer and Doritos. No, those six-pack abs don't simply appear on your gut, and you don't wake up after decades of military dictatorship and discover you have—surprise!—democratic institutions. And even when you've got them, you can never quite be sure what those Supreme Court Justices are doing under those black robes.

3. Papal Supremacy

The Christians, who were white guys done up in a lot of velvety drapes and wild hats,[1] created this system, which basically took the point of view that Christian white guys were the earthly ambassadors of God, that the pope was God's guy on this planet, and if savages, Jews and heathens didn't like it, off with their heads! Best exemplified by the sacking of Jerusalem in 1100, which was apparently a bloodbath that makes Baghdad today seem like St. Tropez in the springtime.

4. Absolute Monarchy, or Those Were the Days My Friend

Although the pope was God's guy on Earth, our vast planet still required a lot of exploring and—but of course—conquering.

Many parts of the world only respond to conquering.

Kings were a lot like corporate CEOs: they took all the money, didn't provide much in the way of health care, then claimed it was for the good of the country. If they'd had a stock market in the Middle Ages, there undoubtedly would have been some royal business commentator recommending that the serfs load up on royalty futures in the short term, and royalty futures in the long term, too, neglecting to mention that he was being paid by the King to dispense this advice.

This political system was popular for many centuries, particularly among members of the aristocracy, who felt that agreeing with whatever the king said beat the living hell out of plowing fields, tending sheep or inventing the industrial revolution for a living (see current ruling Saudi government).

As a result, a large contingent of boozy, stage-trained British actors with great voices—people like Oliver Reed, Richard Burton, Helen Mirren, every Redgrave sister, Cate Blanchett,[2] Ian Holm,

---

1. Foreshadowed the pimp hat.
2. Aussie.

Russell Crowe,[3] Geoffrey Rush[4] and Anthony Hopkins[5]—played kings and queens in movies that got nominated for a *ton* of Oscars, causing many of them to be knighted by the real queen. The trend may have reached its nadir with *The Libertine* (2006), a Johnny Depp movie about the sixteenth-century European aristocracy that is filled with unsavory characters, lots of castle interiors, muddy roads, opera scenes, floppy boobs and poor personal hygiene.

5. Military Dictatorship, Reality Bites and We Shoot Critics on Sight

These are generally the result of too many generations of kings and queens keeping everything for themselves. Unfortunately for kings and queens, they need armies to maintain order, and armies need weapons.

One day, the guy running the army wakes up in a bit of a cranky mood and thinks, what the *hell* am I doing, waking up every morning to go beat the hell out of peasants and savages? What the *hell* am I doing, sailing across a treacherous ocean without so much as a citrus fruit to stem my stinging gums to discover new lands just so the king and queen will have more places to stick their little toy flags when they play Spin the Globe at their next royal dinner party? The king and queen aren't the ones ducking arrows and spears from the savages every time we need to dock the boat and go kill dinner. I have a better idea: I think I'll dock the boat and go kill the king.

And he did. And thus the military dictatorship was born. This is a form of political system the white guy can easily appreciate, although it has fallen from favour amongst most white guys these days since the advent of the videocassette recorder, the United Nations, Amnesty International, PEN and all those pussy liberals

---

3. Aussie.
4. Aussie! Christ, what is it with these Aussies?
5. If he didn't play a king or queen he ought to have.

who don't understand that what people really long for is strength in their leaders.

It didn't help that some of the most recent military dictators, people such as those Argentinean generals, Pinochet and those Serbians, were all pretty loathsome individuals prone to genocidal rages and a lack of media appeal.[6]

It also hasn't helped that non-white guys around the world, in places such as Liberia and Pakistan, have enthusiastically embraced the military dictatorship. Let me tell you, if you thought there was nothing worse than white guys running military dictatorships, you ought to shop for a summer home in Liberia one year.

6. Communist Regimes

For every foppish, yellow-toothed absolute monarch and every short, hair-trigger tempered military dictator, there is an equally resistant force, featuring Intellectual White Guy, Utopian White Guy, Little-Guy Loving White Guy, Vegan White Guy and Trade Union White Guy, who coalesced into a single entity to create the communist regime.

The communist regime was the product of a lot of bearded German intellectuals like Karl Marx, who moped about the opiates of the masses, owning the means of production and the spiritual corruption of the bourgeoisie.

What this translated into, as we saw over the span of about seven decades, were:

1. Lineups.

2. Housing projects that would have been defaced with a lot of anti-communist regime graffiti if the lineups to buy some paint were not so long that the taggers simply gave up and became communists, too.

---

6. Where is it written that a military dictator can't pluck his eyebrows, and has to have hair that's a cross between that of Liberace and Conan O'Brien? Do bushy eyebrows say, "alpha"?

3. No fresh vegetables.

4. Severe vodka addiction.

5. Country *dachas* for everyone who thought resisting the corruption of the bourgeoisie made perfect sense.

6. Political prison for all the poets and novelists, as opposed to the personal hell of being irrelevant in capitalist regimes.

7. An excellent national hockey team who ignited the passions of Canadians during the 1972 Summit Series—and if you think igniting the passions of Canadians is a piece of cake, you haven't spent much time around Canadians.

Communist regimes came into their own during the earliest part of the twentieth century, when capitalism was especially brutal and appeared to have collapsed with the onset of the Depression.

Communist regimes were popular with communist party officials, who didn't have to stand in lineups, got the best seats at the opera and hockey games and spent all of August at their country *dacha* thinking up new reasons why communism was the political system of the future, despite the lineups, vodka addiction, angry poets and terrible vegetables.

Communist regimes were also extremely popular with French and British intellectual white guys who tended to be bad at soccer, smokers and lousy lays and needed a reason to feel superior to the other guys in class. Communist regimes were also quite popular in the U.S. and Canada, particularly among young white guys who were in favour of anything that pissed off their dads, and screenwriters mistreated by studio heads.

This led, just after World War II, to the rise of the "communist witch hunts," during which many lives were ruined by Senator Joseph McCarthy, an alcoholic white guy from Wisconsin bitter about the winters and Wisconsin women.

Eventually, communist regimes ended when the U.S. came to a stunning realization: rather than out-bomb a communist regime, you simply outspend them. Since they were sort of set up to break even on the economy, they couldn't possibly match Capitalist

White Guy when it came to building bombs. The lineups got longer, the vegetables less fresh, the vodka addictions worse and the novels and poems ever more anti-communist. The only thing that stayed the same was the excellence of the Russian national hockey team, which featured Vladislav Tretiak, Valery Kharlamov, Vladimir Petrov and a bunch of other guys NHL owners drooled over.

The year 1980 marked the official turning point in the demise of the communist regime: this was the year Ronald Reagan was elected, and also the year the U.S. Olympic hockey team defeated the Russians at Lake Placid. It was one thing to be starved to death, politically terrorized and denied the opportunity to express yourself at any level. Those things you could grow used to. What was *unacceptable* was losing to American White Guy at ice hockey. That was when Communist White Guy everywhere woke up and said, *whoa Nellie!* This party is *over!* Of course it took another ten years to figure out how to end it, because as everyone whose dad had a lifetime subscription to *Time* knows, communists never did anything in a timely manner—not even collapse.

7. The All-Time Worst White Guy Idea Ever: Apartheid Regimes, or Another Bad Dutch Idea

Everyone has a bad idea once in a while. When I was eighteen, I travelled to Morocco, my first time in the Third World. The first rule of travel in the Third World is, "don't drink the water," because the digestive tracts of First World people can't handle the bacteria and other crunchy stuff that turns up in the drinking water of the Third World. We lack the proper antibodies, or something like that. Of course, possessed as I was with an eighteen year old's fragmentary sense of information, I somehow got the idea that the way to acquire antibodies—much like the way to fight the flu—was to acquire a few strains of bacteria, at which point my body would acclimatize itself to the new realities of Moroccan drinking water.

Terrible idea.

But no one has had as many bad ideas as the Dutch. The Dutch, who in my experience are pretty easygoing, live-and-let-live types, are reputed to have invented Apartheid, when Dutch White Guy woke up in deepest, darkest, resource-rich Africa, found himself wickedly outnumbered, and got an idea: what if Africans didn't count as people?

That would make us the people in charge around here.

And thus, the really, really bad, stupid, evil idea of Apartheid was born.

Apartheid was the idea that white guys and non-white guys can live parallel, but completely separate lives in the same place. Furthermore, one group could own the resources (white guys), have access to the institutions (white guys) and live in the homes with the best views (white guys), while everyone else (non-white guys, who they broke into various categories) could live on substantially less (twigs and seeds), work at poorly paying jobs recovering those resources they didn't own (diamonds and gold) and have no access to institutions.

I have white South African in-laws and a non-white wife, which you might think would make for some tense family gatherings. Actually, it does, but what family gathering doesn't feature an undercurrent of fearful tension? In that, I would say ours are no different from every family in the world.

The truth is, we almost never talk about Apartheid. Let me tell you, the old rule of thumb that families should never talk about politics or religion at the dinner table comes in handy every time we traipse over to Thanksgiving with the fam.

MEL HAS A (white) South African friend too, named Joanne. We used to visit Joanne whenever she was in L.A. visiting her parents, who were really cool. Her mom was studying to be a rabbi. Her dad Bernie was an architect. After a few drinks, they would bring out the Apartheid memorabilia. They didn't hesitate.

One of the things they had was a map of the beach by Cape-town. That might sound sort of dull; just a big patch of sand, right? Wrong.

An apartheid beach is broken into a dozen different stripes. Each one is designated for a different race. There's one stripe for "whites," one for "coloureds" and another for "blacks." I'm pretty sure there were none for "group play," although the parents used to party with non-white guys (and invite the secret police—who would stake out their parties—in for drinks), and on Sunday, they would all go down to the beach together, creating the awkward social dilemma of which strip of sand to lie on.

"Oh, we would all lie on the white part," Bernie (he was white) said. "It was the nicest part of the beach."

What happened?

"No one ever hassled us," he said, "but you would hear stories." Then he would sip his drink and swallow. "But at some point, you know, you have to live your life."

I WONDER WHAT it's like to be that guy, Afrikaaner President of South Africa Guy, F.W. de Klerk, the morning he wakes up—say, a Thursday—has his coffee, reads the Apartheid box scores while eating his Apartheid corn flakes, when the wife asks what he has on tap for the day.

"Honey," he says. "I am going to end Apartheid."

"Can't that wait until next week?"

"Apartheid is a fundamentally evil idea that needs to go away."

"Do you have any idea what that will do to property values?"

"It's morally reprehensible."

"Who will come to clean the pool Wednesdays, Freddie? Who will trim the trees on Friday? How will we divide up the sand on the beach if you end Apartheid? Are you saying people will just be able to lie wherever they feel like it, like Americans or something?"

"Something like that."

"Well, I think it's a terrible idea, but you're the President. It might get you a Nobel, but I will never forgive you."

Chapter Summary

White guys always have a theory about what will work, but the bottom line is that what works is when white guys are in charge.

WHITE GUYS AROUND THE WORLD

· · ·

I T'S A BIG, BIG world, isn't it? And no matter which corner of it you navigate, chances are you will stumble across a few white guys, sitting in a faux-English pub, nursing a pint and gloating over the fact that the weather is better than back home in Brighton, Düsseldorf or Calgary.

White guys come in many shades of pale, including, bizarrely, Green, Brown and Mauve White Guy. In this chapter you'll also meet Expert White Guy, Commuter White Guy, Adventure Travel White Guy, Big Dog Owning White Guy and Bay Area White Guy. Because really, there's no such thing as just one type of anything, and that includes white guys. Thinking we're all exactly the same is as dumb as thinking that every Muslim is a terrorist. No one could be that stupid, right?

Green White Guy

Green White Guy woke up one morning and suddenly it hit him: five thousand years of non-stop progress, and guess what? We overlooked something.

It's called the planet.

Now Green White Guy is trying to make amends to Mother Earth, a little late in the game. The polar ice caps are melting, the Northwest Passage is well on its way to becoming beachfront property, palm trees are popping up in the unlikeliest places and home owners in Phoenix and Australia are wondering if there's another way to say "dry spell," just to break the monotony.

Green White Guy thinks the environment is the single most important issue facing us in the twenty-first century. Big corporations should be held to task for what they've done to the environment—although not at the expense of the economy.

The tricky thing is, to become Green White Guy, you need to have lived in abundance for most of your life. People who were born with nothing don't have the same relationship to abundance that Green White Guy does. They seem to have a hard time embracing the idea that less is better.

The planet might not be in such rough shape if it was just Green White Guys and our loved ones struggling to change our ways, but the fact is, there are whole continents—huge swathes of humankind, like half of China, India and Russia—billions of people still on the first generation of accumulating all that stuff they saw First World White Guy playing with for two thousand years but could never acquire for themselves because of communism, poverty, the czar, feudalism, winter—you know.

Many of those people have spending money now. They have the Bejing Ikea, the New Delhi Home Depot. Many of those sad little Yugos in downtown Moscow have been replaced by Porsches and Mercedes and Hummers. They have cash to burn, and they want their stuff. If you don't, fine. You didn't live in a one-bedroom apartment with seven siblings until the age of twenty-seven because your government believed materialism was wrong.

The rest of the world has some shopping to catch up on. If Green White Guy wants to save the planet by downsizing and simplifying and minimizing himself to the point of invisibility, he can go right ahead. That means fewer competing bids on the monster homes in Kensington and Belgravia and Mayfair, those posh neighborhoods in London that the Russian oligarchs are all moving to.

And then again, many of the greenest white guys around don't live very green lives at all. Once you've had stuff, it's surprisingly hard to go back to less stuff. Once you've put the pedal to the metal, it's sort of tough to put the pedal to the cycle.

Save us from ourselves, Big Al!

Muslim White Guy

Cat Stevens aside, Muslim White Guy (MWG) is a relative rarity, sort of the Stax .45 in the bottom of the box at the yard sale. MWG isn't an oxymoron, but it's kind of strange to open your newspaper, like I did this morning's *National Post*, to see a photo of Richard Heft, 33, a white guy from Winnipeg like me, wearing one of those Muslim robes, with one of those cropped ZZ Top beards and a head wrap with "Erykah Badu" written all over it.

What's up with that?

Of course, MWG surfaced shortly after the invasion of Afghanistan (the American one, not the Soviet one), when John Walker Lindh, a nineteen-year-old from hardscrabble, red dirt, millionaire row Marin County was discovered in a prison yard outside Kabul, in the middle of a riot that resulted in the death of a CIA agent assigned to interrogate the prisoners.

Lindh became a kind of poster child for the War on Terror. He was shipped back to the U.S. and stood trial in Delaware or Virginia or somewhere for sedition, or aiding the enemy during a time of war. The government charged him with everything they could think of, crimes that he could have been sentenced to do ninety years for.

Yikes.

Lindh grew up in Washington, D.C., before moving to Marin County at ten. He was home schooled. He converted to Islam after watching Spike Lee's *Malcom X* at the age of sixteen.

Question: Was it the call of Islam, or did Denzel just look super cool in those skinny ties?

Meanwhile, Manitoba Muslim White Guy Richard Heft is the son of a Lutheran minister. Think he wanted to tick off dad? He went to Iraq to serve as a human shield when the Americans invaded, er, liberated the place. Then he came home. CSIS—the CIA minus the missing torture tapes—interviewed Heft and asked just what the *heck* he was doing in Iraq.

"Jihad," he replied.

Then he changed. He came home to Manitoba. Now, he is still Manitoba Muslim White Guy, but a different brand than the sort of explosives-wearing guy we've grown accustomed to watching on our nightly news. Heft has incorporated a little Canadian moderation into his jihad. He doesn't advocate violence. He tries to teach other young Muslims that suicide bombing the infidels isn't likely to bring back the good old eighth century, when the Muslims ruled the world, any time soon. I don't know if Manitoba Muslim White Guy is a hockey fan on the side, but it wouldn't surprise me.

Brown White Guy, AKA Desi White Guy

Desi White Guy lives in England. He grew up in Hounslow, or one of those grimy neighbourhoods in the British suburbs that have been demographically changed by South Asian immigration. The neighbours where Desi White Guy lives hail from India, Pakistan, Bangladesh—you get the picture. The sons of the parents who moved to the U.K. are grown up now.

The parents, who moved to the U.K. in the '50s and '60s, were deferential, polite—almost more British than British White Guy. That was the way you did it if you were just plain Desi Guy ("Desi" is a Sanskrit word meaning "local," i.e., from East Asia). According to novelist Gautam Malkani, the term for this sort of non-white guy is "coconut": brown on the outside, white on the inside.

But the story has changed for the new generation. Now Desi Guy dresses like a pimp, speaks in a dialect that's a cross between text messaging, hip hop and Cockney, and works out a lot. Desi Guy has his own niche in the London cultural scene, and it ain't a bad one. In fact, by sampling and integrating East Asian, British and American hip hop influences into one unique culture, Desi Guy is really quite the citizen of the world.

So naturally Desi White Guy shows up to claim that he's Desi too.

Markie Mark, a British deejay, is an example of Desi White Guy. He grew up in Hounslow. He plays South Asian records on the BBC and he was even recognized by the South Asian Music Awards in 2003—they gave him an award for his contribution to the South Asian music scene in England.

And the best thing about it is that Desi Guy can live with the fact that there is now Desi White Guy, at least superficially. When I spoke with Malkani, the author of the definitive novel about Desi Guy, *Londonstani*, he talked a lot about how Desi guys use racial and ethnic identity as a proxy for masculine identity, which pretty much sums up a lot of the guys we have been exploring in this chapter, doesn't it? They are all looking for ways to define themselves as guys, and they do it by becoming this kind of white fish out of water.

Although we are all sort of fish out of water these days, when you think about it.

"Everyone can be a Desi now," Malkani says.

That's not quite Martin Luther King's "I Have a Dream" speech, but do you know how much it would cost to text that to your friends?

Everyone Can Be a Desi Now.

College White Guy

All non-white guys and non-white, non-guys have to say about college is, thank God for it. College is where White Guy goes to learn that immigrants do contribute to the economy, that there are other cultures besides American culture, and how to drink astonishing quantities of beer through a plastic tube.

Anything beats running into white guys who spent their late teen years in the bar instead and who now need someone to blame.

College White Guy went to college to learn that there is no validity in the hierarchies of race or gender or class. Then, alas, he joined a frat house, where he learned that the world was built for people like him.

Ten Things You Should Know about College White Guy

10. Secretly would love to rap. In fact, secretly he would love to be from the 'hood—any 'hood but Brentwood.

9. Thinks Asian girls are really hot. Wait. Stop. Thinks almost any girl is really hot.

8. If this stupid frat is such a secret society, why can't he get laid?

7. Would really, really like to give back—as soon as he gets something to give back.

6. He's got a webcam, some roofies, and the dorm to himself Saturday night. Now all he needs is a date.

5. Thought of Facebook six months before that Harvard dude, but didn't know how to write code, so now he works the drive-thru window.

4. Will never, ever follow father into the family business, even if it means working a day job.

3. Owes the campus bookie twenty-two grand for bad NFL bets. Not that it's a problem. He could stop any time he wanted to.

2. Has been writing some songs but is too shy to show them to anyone.

1. Just sold video-downloading website to Fox for $345 million. Paid off campus bookie. Retired at twenty-two. Son of a gun. Anyone want to fly a balloon around the world?

Celebrity Activist White Guy

Nowadays, there is a new kind of helpful W Person: Celebrity Activist White Guy, who, between film shoots, flies to the less savoury parts of the planet and feels the pain of everyone stuck in them. These people have been known to adopt the local children on occasion, so if you are a starving, non-white guy stuck in some thatched hut under a sand dune somewhere, that cloud of dust coming towards you is willing to discuss raising your children in absolute splendour—provided you are willing to sign a non-disclosure pact regarding any discussions with the tabloid press.

The rising popularity of the worst parts of the world as destinations for the most famous people in the world has produced an odd sort of political movement, actually. While no self-respecting news editor would send a film crew to any of these places just to film poor people, it's a whole different kettle of fish when a famous person goes to visit poor people and occasionally adopt their children. Then, it's a story. A feel-good story.

As a result, the world has sat up and taken notice of places it generally spends most of its time trying not to think of, particularly places that manufacture the world's jogging shoes, jeans and fake Rolexes at pennies on the dollar.

Celebrity Activist White Guy might be a hybrid of the sort. He may or may not be slightly crazy, or emotionally misguided. But what the hell: between NGO White Guy and Celebrity Activist White Guy and Angelina Jolie, it's hard not to feel as if things are looking up for Africa.

Five Celebrity Activist White Guys . . .

1. Bono. The true pope. Arguably the world's most powerful man.
2. George Clooney. The true James Bond—only his secret is that he wants to change the world for the better, end injustice and make well-written movies. Maybe the first two, but come on, George.
3. Brad Pitt. Nice, Midwestern, hunky Angelina baggage-schlepper *extraordinaire*.

4. Matt Damon. *People* magazine's Sexiest (Short) Man Alive, who is actually reasonably well-adjusted for a Hollywood celebrity.
5. Leonardo DiCaprio. Much greener white guy than he was as a child star on *Growing Pains*. Al Gore wishes he had Leo's waistline.

. . . and Five Celebs We Wish Were Activists:

1. Don Cherry. You've gotta bodycheck poverty into the ground!
2. Paul Wolfowitz. My name is Paul. I ran the World Bank. You need to help yourself. I have a girlfriend who works at the World Bank to look after.
3. Will Ferrell. Playing a Kenyan marathon runner in his next sports-themed comedy.
4. Hugh Grant. This desert wind does great things to my hair. Where do I go to get fellated?
5. Tony Blair. It's the New Poverty. And we're going to lick it! Unless the Americans say not to.

Big Dog Owning White Guy

BDOWG doesn't feel threatened by the world. He just wants a little insurance. In the case of BDOWG, insurance comes with four legs, a spiked collar and a jaw that could compress rusty, abandoned tanks into manageable strips of recyclable aluminum in no time flat.

Not that the big dog that BDOWG owns is actually much of a threat. No way! The big dog's big secret is that he's pretty much a sweetheart. He might have been abandoned by his first owner in a field just outside Vegas, but nine months of love and tenderness and stable home life pretty much guarantee he won't bite.

Well. Unless you make eye contact. Unless you gesture suddenly in my direction. Or sometimes, he mistakes small children for a threat and mauls them. If that happens, punch him in the nose. He'll let go. Honest. He's not really a danger to anyone, and he's all BDOWG's got in the world, a world that forgot to love him.

Mauve White Guy

One in every twenty white guys is Gay White Guy. That's a lot of guys. At the same time, nineteen out of twenty white guys aren't, and are generally anxious about the one that it is, in case it's secretly them.

Gay White Guy almost doesn't think of himself as a white guy, because he spends a lot of time among white guys feeling anxious or isolated or threatened by guys who look like him, speak like him, but don't quite dress like him or work out like him or drink at the same bars as him.

Call it the theatre community.

Of course, even as there are Gay White Guys at every level of society feeling alienated from the white guy world at large, there are also large numbers of non-white guys and non-guys who see Gay White Guy and just see... a white guy. A cute, cut, well-dressed, funny white guy who makes a lot of money and isn't a pushy bastard.

That's when they usually put two and two together.

Gay White Guy might hate white guys too, but he's one of us— the one who plays us so well in the movies and makes us seem hipper, and wittier, than most of us will ever be.

Five Gay White Guys We Love

1. Tennessee Williams. Author of *A Streetcar Named Desire*; the man who made New Orleans famous on the stage.
2. Truman Capote. Author of *In Cold Blood* and *Breakfast at Tiffany's*.
3. Rupert Everett. Julia Robert's friend in *My Best Friend's Wedding*. Handsome, visciously catty, angry, frustrated actor who speaks the subtext—always a treat.
4. Larry Kramer. A New York original, the author of *The Normal Heart*, and the cranky pants who called out the nation when AIDS erupted in the early '80s in New York City.

5. Sir Ian McKellen. Iconic British actor, came out at forty-eight. Played Gandalf the Grey in *The Lord of the Rings* trilogy. When Sir Ian speaks, E.F. Hutton listens.

Webcam White Guy

Has a DSL connection, a dark room and a valid credit card number. Webcam White Guy lives online. That's where his friends are. That's where his games are. And that's where his relationships are—if you can call someone you pay $4.95 a month to follow your typed instructions a relationship.

Webcam White Guy is alienated in one way. He has no actual life. But in another way, he's a sort of contemporary prototype. He's the most modern man of all. He has a community. He doesn't feel lonely, unless he loses his DSL hookup. He doesn't feel bored, unless he finds himself trapped in front of the TV. He doesn't over-consume, particularly. He doesn't have to. You can download almost everything you need off the Net.

You could almost say this guy leaves the lightest footprint of them all on the planet.

Webcam White Guy's tastes frequently veer towards the sordid, the sick and the downright creepy, because that's the only way he can continue to enjoy his virtual world. It needs to get nastier and nastier, until nothing but sodomized seniors and beheaded alleged terrorists will do the trick.

Webcam White Guy's Virtual Colleagues

1. Gamer White Guy has got his headphones, his Red Bull and his competitive drive. There are leagues of gamers now. How long until ESPN is televising Gamer White Guy mouse-clicking his way to global domination?

2. Sports Blog White Guy wants the coach fired. Whoever the coach is. He is the problem. He must go. What the team needs is a shake-up. A major trade. Particularly a major trade in which

your team gives up its scrubs at the end of the bench for some other team's disgruntled, reasonably paid superstar. Oh, wait. I forgot. There are none of those, any more.

3. **Political Conspiracy White Guy** knows that Bush caused 9/11. He has the files to prove it. It was financed by the oil industry so that they could get their pipeline built in Afghanistan. You would have to be naive to think otherwise. Has anyone seen my meds?

4. **Canadian Pharmaceutical Senior White Guy:** "I'll be god-damned if I'm going to spend the final twenty years of my life financing some Merck a-hole's yearend bonus. Buy some bus tickets, and pack the passports, Millie. We're riding up to Winnipeg."

5. **Baby Picture White Guy** has a mailing list of hundreds of people he barely knows who will be ecstatic to receive forty-four pictures of his child's first day, forty-four pictures of his child's second day, forty-four pictures of his child checking out of the hospital. As an added bonus, there are 132 pictures of his wife after not sleeping for eighty hours, thirty-five pounds overweight. Who needs a webcam when you've got Baby Picture White Guy?

Adventure Travel White Guy

Adventure Travel White Guy has been around for twenty-three or twenty-four centuries. Adventure travel white guy existed before adventure travel. Adventure travel white guy even existed before books!

Pre-books, Adventure Travel White Guy lived in places like Spain, Italy, France and particularly England, where unless you were in tight with the king and his court, island-living could get a little oppressive. English Adventure Travel White Guy also tended to be handy in a boat, which was the predominant form of transport in those days, and in a fight, you couldn't go wrong taking English Adventure Travel White Guy, particularly if the opponent was French White Guy, who was generally eager to sign a treaty with whoever wanted to fight him.

English Adventure Travel White Guy was always travelling off on eighteen-month, around-the-world voyages to discover the New World, the Northwest Passage, the South Seas—stuff like that. To tell you the truth, it's been all downhill since English Adventure Travel White Guy did all that stuff, although I guess Spanish white guy got the writing credit on the New World.[1]

Cut to the present. The world has shrivelled. Companies have branch offices all over it. So does Starbucks. You can sit on a plane for twenty-three hours, catch a cab to the Days Inn, sleep, wake up and still have a *venti* drip and inedible pastry for breakfast, just as if you hadn't left home.

It might be a great time to be a corporation, but it sort of sucks to be Adventure Travel White Guy.

I mean, imagine being that guy. Imagine being the guy who goes where no W Person has gone before. Aside from Mars, a few dodgy parts of major American cities, and Jedda, there's not much left, is there? All the passages have been passed. All the English Channels have been swum. All the peaks ascended.[2]

Adventure Travel White Guy has ridden the train from Boston to Patagonia (Paul Theroux), traversed Arabia's Empty Quarter (Sir Wilfred Thesiger), hopped the bus from Cairo to Capetown (Theroux again) and walked across the Australian outback the way the Aboriginals once did (Bruce Chatwin). He has hiked the entire Appalachian Trail despite being white, a guy, overweight and fiftysomething (Bill Bryson). He has been to both poles (Roald Amundsen) and even dragged a film crew around the world in

---

1. Screenwriter gallows humour. L.A. flashback. Sorry about that.
2. The Darien Gap, which connects Central to South America, is an eighty-kilometre isthmus that is still relatively unexplored. It's filled with malarial mosquitoes and Columbian guerillas who are fond of taking people hostage. There is also some sort of oil industry presence there—of course there is!

eighty days, and from pole to pole, full circle, and across the Sahara and the through the Himalayas (Michael Palin).

All of which is a roundabout way of asking, Why? Why do Adventure Travel White Guys do it?

That's what all those Sherpas sit around talking about, as they wait for the next batch of rich W People to arrive at base camp armed with fistfuls of cash in order to be led up to the summit of Everest.

As Melanee once famously observed after I nearly died climbing Mt. Whitney, the highest peak in the continental U.S., even though I don't, as a rule, climb mountains, and really just got macho one Sunday: "You'd have to be white in the first place to think climbin' a mountain is fun. You don't see black people up on a mountain, because black people's lives are hard enough without them climbing a mountain for fun."

Meanwhile, with the world shrinking and *The Da Vinci Code* opening on the same day in Kathmandu that it opened in L.A., the opportunities to be that fish-out-of-water adventure guy have been reduced to almost nil.

In fact, I'd say it's time for Adventure Travel White Guy to turn his gaze inward, upon himself. Maybe all that's left, the only real terrain we haven't yet explored up close and personal, is the terrain we spent the past thirty centuries developing. It's our mess. Maybe hiding underneath it, there's the secret to life.

Ten Places Adventure Travel White Guy Still Hasn't Gone

10. A year in West Edmonton Mall. Twelve months of retail hell.
9. A walk on the Autobahn. Travels on German superhighways.
8. Cul-de-whacked. Living in the suburbs with a family of four and their plasma TVs.
7. Luxury box. Sitting through every event for one calendar year at Staples Center, including every WNBA game played by the Los Angeles Sparks.

6. Cruise ship. Going around the world, listening to Old Retired White Guy's stories on a Carnival Cruise Lines trip without wanting to kill yourself.

5. Baseball season. Living off ballpark food for an entire season's worth of Baltimore Orioles games.

4. Being Steve Jobs. In which we get to spend a year being a billionaire who wears jeans and sneakers to work and thinks up brilliant new gadgets.

3. Watching every late night talk show starring Late Night White Guy Comic and trying to tell us the difference. Why don't they all just team up like the *Best Damn Sports Show* on Fox? They could call it *Best Damn Late Night Talk Show* starring *A Half Dozen White Guys With Remarkably Similar World Views*.

2. Staying home with toddler while mom works. And living to write a book about it.

1. I was a YouTube sensation one morning when I was twenty. And now I need to somehow turn that fifteen seconds of infamy into a career.

Commuter White Guy

Commuter White Guy spends a very large chunk of his life in transit. The form of transit varies; it might be a commuter train, a subway or a city bus, but chances are good, if you're North American White Guy, it's an automobile, and it's just you, your cell phone, your radio and forty-five minutes if you hit all the lights and there weren't any accidents on the expressway.

Commuter White Guy is a direct result of Suburban White Guy, who lives on the outskirts of the city and works on the inskirts.

Upside: owning an oversized chunk of house beyond anything your parents ever dreamed of owning.

Downside: 20 per cent of your week spent coming and going.

The deep, dark secret here is that Commuter White Guy loves his commute. Sure, he says all the right things whenever the conversation turns to the commute, but secretly, it's his time—time he wouldn't give up for anything. He has kids, a wife, a boss and obligations. His life is way overscheduled. He has no "me time," except for those forty-five minutes each way, to reflect upon life, to ask the questions that need to be asked, to make long-term and short-term plans or at least to phone in to complain about the Flames power play, or Isiah Thomas or immigration issues (maybe Angry White Guy with his racial scapegoating is nothing more than Commuter White Guy with low blood sugar stuck in gridlock).

Yes, it would be better for all involved—the flow of traffic, the environment, the very-well being of the planet if every Commuter White Guy just kept the car parked in the garage and hoofed it to the light rail station in the morning. And in theory, a lot of Commuter White Guys are in favour of this. Just as long as it doesn't involve them.

They're addicted to their car.

Then there are those days when it all goes to hell and the forty-five minutes turns into seventy-five, or ninety, or two hours. Or there are the Extreme Commuters that Nick Paumgarten wrote about in a great story in *The New Yorker*, people who travel three hours each way, every day. They're absolutely crazy—either that, or they're a cross between Adventure Travel, Overachieving and Commuter White Guy, all blended into the same $300 suit he should have thrown out two spring cleanings ago.

Six Whitest Commutes in the World

6. **The 401 to downtown Toronto.** Nothing says Commuter White Guy quite like watching the exits fill up with sensible four-door sedans as Commuter White Guy flees Mississauga for a day in the trenches.

5. **8:15 Metro North from Tarrytown to Grand Central.** Competing only with the 5:45 Metro North from Grand Central back to Bronxville, which features the added attraction of a mixed drink and a nice relaxing game of speed checkers with the boys.

4. **Eastbound on Olympic Boulevard (Los Angeles) at 9:45 AM**
When all the show-business suits are stuck on Olympic, phones glued to their ears as they berate their assistants for causing the traffic to be so bad.
3. **Any highway in Salt Lake City, around rush hour.** Things get busy when you have to race home to see the wive(s).
2. **The RER to downtown Paris.** It would be ideal if they just skipped every stop until the Fifth Arrondissement so all of the Senegalese and Algerians and Moroccans would be forced to walk.
1. **I-5 south anytime.** Orange County, the prosperous region south of Los Angeles, north of San Diego and zip code to the highest-average house prices in the nation, has long been maligned for being a bastion of right-wing conservatism; overlooking the fact that Santa Ana is completely full of non-white guys, that's basically right on the money.

Anti-War White Guy, AKA Bay Area White Guy

For every prevailing force, there is a counter prevailing reaction. Among Americans, this guy is more commonly known as Bay Area White Guy, or MoveOn.org White Guy. Bay Area White Guy owes everything he's got—his seven-figure home, his low-percentage body fat, his impressive wine cellar (who knew a former radical could have such a collection of shiraz?), his career, his (third) marriage, his far-too-mainstream-for-his-taste, establishment-loving children, his general erudition—to a lifetime spent being against shit.

Bay Area White Guy was against Vietnam, against corporate greed, against building interstate highways, against real estate development (but he never said anything about rehabilitating Haight-Ashbury walkups; who knew that would make him a multimillionaire?). Bay Area White Guy was against cars, against racism, against AM radio, against Hollywood, against media mergers, against regulating the Internet, and who knew the thousand shares of Yahoo! stock he bought the day of the IPO would put three kids through college?

Bay Area White Guy is against L.A., which goes without saying, and still gets a tingle every time the Giants beat the Dodgers, even though he is against baseball, because sport is the opiate of the masses. Bay Area White Guy is against celebrity, and wishes there were rules against those horrible people even existing. He is against tech in general and believes the world would be better off if we all just got to know our community better, although he does love the email and the blog. He is dead set against the pharmaceutical industry, who he considers just this side of war criminals, although he did get quite a life from going on Paxil for six months after the second wife left with the contractor who fixed up the Haight-Ashbury place.

Okay, he's even against people like him, but that's the one thing that makes him different from everyone else in this chapter: irony.

Bay Area White Guy got rich being against shit.

Is it a great country or what?

Of course, now that he has hit his prime years and become a member of the economic, social and political mainstream, Bay Area White Guy is more against shit than ever. Being against shit made him rich; why can't kids today see that being against shit is the best way to get anywhere in this stinking, corrupt, materialistic, celebrity-driven culture? You want someone to notice the brand you're pushing, even if that brand is you?

Be against it!

These are a return to the glory days of a sort for Bay Area White Guy. What with the kids off to their media industry internships, the wife on her national yoga tour that grosses more than most bands could ever dream about, and the bank account full, Bay Area White Guy has taken to blogging his thoughts about all the things he's against.

And what do you know?

Millions of people across the country are just as against shit as he is.

Expert White Guy, AKA British Empire White Guy II

Expert White Guy is that guy on the cable news, explaining what went wrong. It doesn't particularly matter what went wrong. It might be a war, might be a hurricane, might be a steroid scandal, might even be a Russell Crowe temper tantrum, but whatever it is, there is an Expert White Guy available to appear on TV and explain.

Expert White Guy speaks in declarative sentences. He is certain about whatever it is he is certain about. There's no middle ground, no grey area, no other side's point of view to consider when you're on TV playing Expert White Guy. This has to do less with whoever is playing Expert White Guy and more to do with what television producers want from their experts. It wants someone, preferably someone with hair, ideally someone hot but someone with hair will do, to be certain of something, because at times of crisis, viewers need comforting and there is nothing more comforting than Expert White Guy explaining how it's not our fault that any of these horrible things are happening.

Nowadays, there is Expert Non-White Guy and Expert Non-Guy as well, in order to provide a lively ethnic and gender balance to the conversation, although to tell the truth, the best way to become Expert Non-White Guy and Expert Non-Guy is usually to become Expert White Guy in disguise.[3]

The number one British export over the last century has probably been Expert White Guys, chaps who weren't quite experts on the home front, so they flooded out into the provinces and the U.S., where it will do if you speak with one of those Oxbridge accents and have good posture and one of those rumpled tweed blazers.

Nowadays, however, even Expert White Guy isn't quite what he used to be. *The Daily Show* has a resident Expert White Guy, John Hodgman, who's either a fake expert or an expert on everything.

---

3. Condoleezza if you please. Also, Laura Ingram and Ann Coulter.

He just plays one on the fake daily news! It's appalling, what little regard those people have for expertise.

AM Radio White Guy

Every tribe has its community leaders. African-Americans have preachers. Latin Americans have strongmen. Dominicans have shortstops who sign guaranteed $60-million deals with large-market ball clubs, then come home and fix the baseball diamonds in their hometowns.

White guys have AM Radio White Guy.

AM Radio White Guy is the first voice you hear in the morning. He gets up before everyone, even the milkman. AM Radio White Guy is funny. He says provocative things in order to get listeners to call in, because if you say unprovocative things, you end up with a nice middle of the afternoon show no one listens to.

AM Radio White Guy comes in different flavours, but pretty much only one colour. The archetype is Don Imus. The I-Man is the original angry white guy, but now, at sixty-something, he's mellowed, even if he did call those Rutgers basketball players "nappy-headed 'hos."

He used to be way worse.

And popular. The I-Man begat Howard Stern, who begat a generation of shock jocks such as Opie and Anthony, not to mention someone in almost every radio market on the air trying to find the edge of whatever envelope they're pushing that day.

Rush Limbaugh is AM Radio White Guy Eminence, and is often credited with single-handedly saving AM radio. A former sports publicist from the Midwest, Rush is a disgruntled white guy angry with the direction the country is moving in, if you get the subtext (women, non-white guys, liberal values, national health care).

Oh wait. Thanks to the revolution Rush and Newt started, the country is no longer moving in any of those directions! In fact, the country is moving in the direction Rush always implied it should move in: religious, rightward, military-driven, privatized, anti-immigrant, paranoid, borders closed, shutting out the rest of the world, everyone a homeowner and a gun owner and a season-ticket holder and hopefully your team doesn't start a black quarterback like Donovan McNabb, who is so overrated.

You might say guys like Rush changed the face of the (American) nation.

There are lots of mini-Rushes now, guys like Joe Scarborough, Sean Hannity and Laura Ingram, who is not technically a guy but pretty well plays one on the radio. She's funny, blonde, smart and right-wing as hell.

In L.A., there's even Jesus. He's got a show on KFI 640, the most popular talk radio station in town, every Sunday morning. Jesus is played by Neil Saavedra, a former punk rock drummer from Orange County. L.A. Jesus is actually one of the more reasonable Jesuses you're likely to run into, and thanks to his musical background, the show has great musical "bumps" into and out of each segment.

Canada has its homegrown versions of AM Radio White Guy, such as Charles Adler, heard nationally out of the studios of CJOB in Winnipeg. But if you ask me, the true radio conversation in Canada is to be heard on the CBC's national programs such as *As It Happens* and *Definitely Not the Opera*. These shows tend to be hosted by non-guys such as Barbara Budd and Carol Off, journos with no-nonsense attitudes and voices that drip with sarcasm. One of my favourite things to do is to turn on the radio while I'm making dinner after a long day and listen to CBC non-guys talking to the world. It's so much different than listening to the radio in the U.S., where for the most part, the world stops at the American border.

AM Radio White Guys are the community leaders. They start the conversations in the morning. They wake everyone up. And they need right angles to make their discussions sharper. AM Radio doesn't handle shades of grey very well; it likes villains and heroes, sort of like Hollywood movies. People are either idiots or demons, criminals or saviors. Immigration is a threat, and when people feel threatened, guess what?

They call in!

Road Trip White Guy

So who, you may well ask, listens to AM Radio White Guy?

CUT TO:

He can be found loitering inside truck stops, which these days are filled with Christian books, NASCAR sponsor ball caps—Napa Auto Parts, M&Ms and the rest—and racks of jerky sold in bulk. There are donuts and hot sandwiches and cassette tapes that offer soft hits from the '70s that I am ashamed to say I like (old Doobie Brothers, America, the Eagles).

I hate it when that happens.

Road Trip White Guy loves the freedom of the open road, even when it isn't particularly open (Willie Nelson needs to write a song about eating a ciabatta bacon-and-egg sandwich at Jack in the Box at 7 AM just outside Sacramento). Road Trip White Guy often drives a white pickup truck, the better to peer down at Arts Journalist White Guy, who had the insane idea of driving to Canada so he could have his two-decade-old car there. Road trip white guy drives alone.

Road Trip White Guy is nothing but lines on his face. Road Trip White Guy looks like he's spent thirty years sleeping sitting up in the cab of his semi. Road Trip White Guy is maybe fifty-five, but looks seventy-five. He wears baggy-assed, old-man jeans, a ball cap and a team jacket. Today it is the Sacramento Kings.

You know that guy in high school, the one who had the ugly mom and the hateful dad? The guy who was absolutely doomed from the moment he arrived on earth?

That guy became a trucker.

Truck stops are filled with that guy, a torn-up white guy looking for a conversation, because let's face it, driving a truck is a lonely life, particularly when you look like Road Trip White Guy always looks. A hat of some sort—and for sure not a jaunty, New York-style fedora. You tuck in your shirt—and rest assured, it's a hideous shirt. A prominent belt, with a substantial buckle—there's no such thing as an insubstantial buckle when you're Road Trip White Guy.

Overachiever White Guy

No matter what he does, Overachieving White Guy does it a little longer and a little more in-depth than you do. Overachieving White Guy stays later at the office, or rises earlier in the morning. Overachieving White Guy even surfs higher waves, works out longer or relaxes more intensely than you.

You might look at surfer Laird Hamilton and see the epitome of a California guy, the blond, handsome surfer from the Beach Boy songs, but make no mistake about it: this is Twenty-First Century Surfer Guy, not 1960s Surfer Guy. That surfer guy hung out in the sand, smoked weed, bagged rays, listened to tunes, cruised chicks and waited for the perfect wave. He lived in a shack not far from the ocean down in Laguna. He perfected living in the moment. He drove a VW bus that had no reverse, so every time he had to back out of a parking lot, he had to gather up his pals and push. Life was a blast.

Now Laguna is known as the town "where the billionaires have kicked out the millionaires." It's the setting of a popular reality show, about prematurely sophisticated teenagers charting their career arcs.

Laird Hamilton surfer guy doesn't live in Laguna. He lives in Hawaii. He doesn't hang out in the sand. He trains by diving under the water with huge rocks strapped to his legs. He's an industry, a media icon. He has corporate sponsors. He goes on TV. He does all the things Twenty-First Century Corporate Icon Guy does. The sportswear company Billabong pays Hamilton to surf the world's biggest waves, which surface just outside his house. Surfers, dilettantes and guys who just wanna get on TV descend on Hawaii whenever these big waves are reported to be in the area. There's big money to be made in surfing now, just like there's big money to be made in just about every single fun thing American guy ever did, whether it's skateboarding, strumming a guitar, hitting a baseball, shooting hoops or telling jokes. There's nothing a guy can do to amuse himself these days without being aware that if it all works out, he could earn millions!

And so fun becomes work.

QUESTION: *when fun becomes work, what does an overachieving white guy do for fun?*

ANSWER: *Don't bug me. I'm busy.*

Hip Hop Outcasts, AKA The Wigger

(Note: Not to be confused with Outkast, the Hip Hop group)
There is a long, profitable tradition of white guys appropriating the musical stylings of non-white guy and making a killing.

In rough chronological order, there's Elvis, Jerry Lee Lewis, The Rolling Stones, the Yardbirds, Led Zeppelin, KC and the Sunshine Band, Paul Simon, Peter Gabriel, Tom Waits, the Backstreet Boys, Vanilla Ice, The Beastie Boys, Eminem, all the way up to K-Fed, the poor, beleaguered ex-husband of Britney Spears. There's even a Christian wigger: Manafest, a rapper I saw perform at the 2007 Gospel Music Awards. He was kind of fun.

The Inner Life of Wiggers

See *Interlude A: The Quest for Authenticity* (p. 93)

Mercenary White Guy

The Iraq War, it's safe to say, has been an astonishing fiasco. And while war is, for the most part, a fiasco for Non-White Grunt Guy, one of the more surprising aspects of this one, which I discovered reading Paul Roberts Williams' excellent *The War against Truth*, a memoir of the war's first months, is that there are an abundant number of white guy grunts fighting this one—short, undernourished, uneducated white guys who got sold a story by the Bush administration about fighting terrorists, and bit.

This isn't about those guys.

Mercenary White Guy is something else entirely. He's Erik Prince, the richest person ever to enroll in the U.S. Army, the scion of Blackwater, a Michigan-based private security firm who have been reaping the benefits of global chaos in places like Iraq, New Orleans and now Darfur, where they are pitching themselves as private peacekeepers willing to chopper in to halt the genocide.

The Prince family are evangelical Christians who, following the Columbine massacre in Littleton, Colorado, built a simulated high school on a ranch in Michigan in order to instruct anxiety-ridden school district supervisors in the finer details of self-defense. When Hurricane Katrina obliterated order in New Orleans, Blackwater choppered in guys who ended up securing Wal-Mart parking lots. They earned over $30 million for their work in New Orleans, and no one knows how much they've made in Iraq, where they have been working as a for-hire security army who frequently find themselves in firefights with the locals.

Mercenary White Guy sees global chaos as a business opportunity. Where you see unspeakable violence and environmental havoc, Mercenary White Guy sees overtime pay. While Toothless Grunt White Guy earns about $1,200 a month and has to buy his plane ticket home from the East Coast and his parents have to launch fundraisers to get him a proper bulletproof vest to fight a pointless war no one except Cheney and Bush still want to fight, Mercenary White Guy works security and clocks two or three grand a week. He doesn't answer to the military. He's well fed. He's in Baghdad this month, down in the Sudan next month.

While the white guy has always been a master at taking global lemons and making money selling the lemonade, it's hard to think of a more reprehensible example than Mercenary White Guy—although Arms Merchant White Guy would be close.

It's almost comforting, in a Mad Max sort of way, to see that, as the twenty-first century unravels and the planet buckles amid environment devastation, government disintegration and wars and plagues without end, there is also a white guy following close behind, finding the business angle behind it all.

Some things never change.

And Finally: Performance Artist White Guy

When I moved to New York in 1989, the one-man show was all the rage. Monologists like Spalding Gray told stories about themselves that were part theatre and part standup comedy. I saw them telling stories that were funny and moving and cool, and thought, that's what I want to do, too!

The problem was to find a subject matter.

A quick survey of the one-man-show scene revealed a few common themes. There was Secretly Gay Monologist—or not so secretly, now that I think about it. There was Emotionally Traumatized Monologist (often traumatized by white guys, or at least a world run by white guys). There was Underemployed Monologist (Claudia Shear), or Lesbian Monologist (Lisa Kron), or a half-dozen Unemployed Actor-Gets Quirky-Job, Learns Lesson About Life Monologists.

You all know where this is leading to: White Guy Monologist! So why linger?

That's where I ended up. I didn't even have Melanee as a racial cover story when I started doing Performance Art White Guy back in 1993. I just did it, in a class full of actors, at the Ensemble Studio Theatre. It was taught by Curt Dempster, the founder of EST. He made this speech to us about how we are very own best material—and the only way you're gonna get anyone's attention, he said, is to tap into whatever is it about you that makes you unique. Then he asked us to write something.

Seven minutes about being straight, white and male. Then I read it to class—and they laughed. They laughed quite a bit.

It was 1993. I thought, I think I've got something here. And then I started to do it around town. I did it at the West Bank Café, the so-called Sardi's of Off-Off Broadway. Did it at Ensemble Studio Theatre any number of times. Every time we were putting together a show over there, Curt would say, in his 1940's mug's voice, "Why don't you do that white guy bit?" I would, and it invariably would kill. Except when I performed it downtown, in the East Village. That's the neighbourhood of Manhattan that was the most bohemian, artsy, avant-garde place around. It was full of cheap restaurants, cool bars, clubs, theatre and pretty girls and parties. And Ukrainians. I'm half-Ukrainian, so when I got homesick for Winnipeg, I just had to go sit in Vesselka and have a bowl of borscht and the blues went away.

The thing of it was, no one wanted to hear from white guys. White guys were what people moved to the East Village to escape from—even white guys moved there to escape from themselves.

There was a popular open mic run by a woman named Ellie. It's probably still going. It used to happen at her space, which she called Dixon Place. It was on Second Street for a while, then on the Bowery. It was kind of the first stop for a lot of monologists working on new material. I did *The White Guy* there one night and remember her listening, the most open-minded, First-Amendment-loving hostess in the East Village. After I'd performed she said, "I'd just like to remind everyone that white guys aren't the only ones who have problems."

(I was going to explain to her that it was ironic, but by then, I figured, the only politic thing to do was to cut and run, before I became known as the least cool guy in the East Village.)

I sent *The White Guy* to PS 122, another one of the major developmental theatres, and never heard a word. It took The Public Theatre—run, no less, by African-American Artistic Director Guy George Wolfe—to produce *The White Guy*.

Only Non-White Theatre Guy would take a chance on Performance Art White Guy.

Because he made white people too nervous.

If there's one racial experience East Village experimental theatre guy didn't want to explore, it was being white, straight and a guy.

Anyways, although it hurt my feelings to be rejected by the East Village theatrical establishment (it didn't help that I couldn't act my way out of a paper bag; I'd hoped that my wooden monotone performing style would come across as a character thing, but it only came across as a wooden monotone performing style; I was, and still am, the Al Gore of performance art), I did take a small degree of comfort in knowing that I'd found a topic that was still taboo in artsy East Village circles, at a time when nothing else was taboo. After Karen Finley shoved that yam up her ass and got a government grant for it,[4] there wasn't a whole lot that got left off the stage in the East Village. Until Performance Art White Guy came along.

Chapter Summary

You see them here, you see them there, those goddamn white guys are everywhere.

---

4. Late '80s performance art technique. It aroused the ire of Congress, who threatened to wipe out funding for the National Endowment of the Arts (NEA) for years thereafter. The NEA has never really recovered from Finley's yam incident.

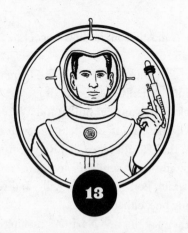

13

TWENTY-FIRST-CENTURY
WHITE GUY

· · ·

WHILE THE PREVIOUS thirty centuries have been filled with somewhat dispiriting examples of white guys at their worst—Henry VIII, Goebbels, "Weird Al" Yankovic—could it be possible that the White Guy is actually improving? Could it be that, after decades of diversification and feminism, we have come out the other end a little more self-aware, a little less self-absorbed, a little more funny and a little more capable of sharing?

On the upside, I have five words: Owen Wilson and Ben Stiller.

Owen Wilson and Ben Stiller are movie actors, and it's always risky to confuse actors with actual people, so maybe we shouldn't even begin to deal with them as real people. Instead, let's look at their personas.

Both are funny, gracious guys who are good listeners. Both understand the appeal of relationships, rather than behaving like one-man bands off In Pursuit of Excellence at the emotional expense of everyone, themselves included. Both are kind of cool, although Stiller is mostly cool for how uncool he is, starting with his enormous ears.

On the downside: Dick Cheney. (Upside: there isn't much time left for Dick to intellectually waterboard us.)

Let's go back to the upside. Stiller and Wilson are the kind of white guys who have no trouble hanging with non-white guys. Both grew up in the U.S. after the Civil Rights struggles had been fought. Both are culturally sensitive, and have travelled and read. Both find non-white, non-guy sexy as hell—and wouldn't have a problem marrying one, either.[1]

Downside: they say the neo-Nazis are making a comeback in Germany.

Upside: they finally blew up Apartheid in South Africa. They held the Truth and Reconciliation Hearings, where all the South African white guys confessed their misdeeds, and received amnesty in return. The white guys handed the reins of the country over to the non-white guys, and somewhat amazingly, the hand-over was fairly peaceful, with no vengeful non-white guys getting violent payback for the past three hundred years. That's no small deal.

Downside: a lot of the white guys live in homes they bought before they ever thought to let Mandela out of jail, surrounded by thirteen-foot-high electric-wired fences, to keep the criminals (subtext: the non-white guys) out. (What's that saying about good fences make good neighbours?)

Upside: the Northern Irish White Guys made peace with the British White Guys.

Downside: the British White Guys decided co-invading Iraq was a good idea.

Upside: Latino mayors in major American cities like Los Angeles, where Latinos are now the dominant population.

Downside: Now the Latinos all want to stay in L.A., so there's no damn good Mexican food in Canada.

---

1. OK. Stiller married a blonde. But a funny blonde.

But what about Ben and Owen? Neither is really Pursuit of Excellence White Guy, either. Both are capable of living with the rampaging, relentless less-than-excellence that life throws at you. Both are just as likely to check into the Motel 6 on their way across the country on some interstate highway as they are to show up in the lobby of the local Four Seasons Hotel. Both, you are convinced, have strong burger tendencies, but are not above a pit stop at the In-N-Out.

Downside: Owen tried to commit suicide.

Upside: He failed! Hey, that's life in L.A.: suicide attempts happen.

Downside: being pro-torture these days is considered realpolitik, while believing in the Geneva Convention is considered hopelessly naive. Did we all beam back to the twelfth century when I wasn't paying attention?

Upside: Jeb is never going to be able to live down Dubya's two terms in office, so the planet may be spared any more of the Bush Dynasty for a few years—at least until Jeb's son grows up.

Upside: The Australian PM said sorry to the Aborigines for all the appalling things Aussie W Guy did to them over the last two centuries.

Downside: No financial settlement for the Aborigines. They're not *that* sorry.

Nevertheless, Stiller and Wilson: two well-above-average (but not too well above) white guys, who also happen to be the archetypal leading men of their generation.

But look at the election campaign we're in right now. After 232 years of white guys steering the ship, America seems to be ready for a non-white, a non-guy (OK, or a war hero) at the helm. It hasn't been pretty. It hasn't been without its centuries of injustice, indignities and just plain old nastiness.

But still. Barack and Hillary in 2008!

How cool is that?

And if it's really, really weird having a non-guy or non-white guy be the president, in 2016 how about Clooney for President?

White People (Secretly) Love Black People

When she isn't obsessing about what the woman at the drugstore thinks about her, Melanee will occasionally observe some sort of intra-racial encounter and say, "See? The truth is that white people actually love black people. They always have. That's why they're so weird about race, because they can't quite come to terms with the feelings they have."

Excuse me?

Isn't the whole subtext of the relationship between white guys and everyone else supposed to be that we secretly hate you?

Could it be, is it possible, is there some way that it's all just been one big *miscommunication?*

I never quite know what to say when she says this. I have spent years and years under the impression that, lurking just under the surface of my psyche, sits this raving, angry racist guy just busting to break free every time I drink a six pack.

In fact, Melanee often has that same conversation with her non-white, non-guy friends who date white guys. There's a common line of thought that says, just wait until he gets angry enough. Sooner or later, every white guy will call you a dirty n–bomb.

But Melanee thinks we secretly love black people. (Does that include wives who leave the lid off everything, and never remember to put gas in the car?)

The other day, she goes, "The truth is that white people have always been really nice to me, for my whole life, but if you're black and say you like white people, it makes you an inauthentic black person."

Hey! They stole that from white guys!

Of course, it isn't all good news when the news turn to race. (For one thing, she has never mentioned a deep, abiding belief that secretly, black people love W's—so we still have a ways to go.)

You know that. Just pick up a daily paper, just about anywhere. There's people hating on each other all the time. Always has been. Always will be.

It helps to remember that people of different races or religions loving each other is always less of a news story. For some mysterious reason, violence makes people reach into their pocket and shell out for a paper. Love? That's not a story. That's a movie plot. That's a ballad. That's a greeting card sentiment. Not a news story.

And just as white guys, who have received decades of training and conditioning and education and reprisals, are learning to relate to all the non-white guys and non-guys on the planet, there's this to consider: Non-white guys hate non-white guys, too.

In Los Angeles, there's all sorts of difficult racial dynamics that have nothing to do with W People. In high schools, there are turf wars between Latino and African-American students, drive-by shootings and threats being issued on the web. All of which might be expected of high school students, but it filters out into the general population, too.

When Melanee goes to a drugstore in Santa Monica, one of the wealthiest communities in America, she gets racially profiled by the security guards and cashiers, who are frequently minorities themselves. She comes home steaming about this. "I went to Bennington College," she says. "I have a university degree. I had a TV series. I did a feature with Kevin Spacey. And then some seven-dollar-an-hour Mexican security guard is following me around a drugstore, to make sure I don't stick some hair relaxer in my purse!"

Then she drops the bomb on them.

"Latinos are the new white people!" she says.

Know what? That's a relief. W People are ready to be something else. We've been W people far too long.

Chapter Summary:

Latinos are the new white people.

OPTIONAL ENDING

— *for* —

PEOPLE WHO DON'T HAVE TIME TO
READ THE WHOLE BOOK

• • •

WE REALIZE THAT books require a commitment of time and mental energy that many people choose not to make these days, what with Facebook, iPhones, saving the environment, *House, The Office, Guitar Hero* and whatnot. Rather than explaining all the reasons why you really ought to read books, we have gone the next best: here, in a few pithy bullet points, is everything I've said in the previous couple hundred pages, boiled down to a few bright and breezy concluding thoughts.

You Know You're a White Guy If . . .

Customs actually believes you thought it was cloves, and tells you to have a nice stay in their country.

You are your own co-signer.

The co-op board thought your application was just fine. You're in.

Someone bombs you, it's terrorism. When you bomb them, it's for their own good.

You get shot by criminals, it makes the front page instead of the City section of the paper.

You really, really want to give back because you've been so fortunate.

Crossing things off your list is your most satisfying act of the day, next to checking your Blackberry and fantasizing about cashing in frequent-flier miles.

You brag about your mileage. And the other guys in the bar actually envy you for it.

You dream of leaving a lighter footprint on the planet and don't find it contradictory that two pints earlier, you were bragging about your mileage.

You've ever dreamed of being a pro bull rider.

Your idea of cool is spending a night at that hotel made of ice in Quebec City.

Vacation time is just another way of saying, "Excellent cardio," and when you hear the words "Degree of difficulty," you actually get erect dreaming of climbing the Seven Summits.

Those days seemed a lot wilder than these days. Before security clearances.

Your idea of understated is owning a sailboat under fifty feet long. And no staff.

You know all the words to more than three Bruce Springsteen songs. How can you not? "Had a wife and kids in Baltimore, Jack / I went out for a ride . . ."

You don't see what's so boring about the missionary position. If it works, it works.

You used to be into death metal, but prefer alt country these days.

Arcade Fire totally rules.

It's nothing a little discipline couldn't solve. Hugging is for when you win the Cup.

The Van Halen reunion tour was your emotional highlight of 2007. But bring back lighters!

You know who won the Stanley Cup and feel a little bitter about it, because those fans don't deserve the Stanley Cup.

You have an opinion on the IRL v. NASCAR.

You can say "camping" without wincing.

There's almost never a moment that a cold beer couldn't improve.

The nut on the radio actually makes sense about: a) Terrorism b) Immigration c) The idiots running the country.

Your deep, dark secret is that you don't really have one.

You use the word "equity" a lot, and actually know what it means—and never use the word "equality" except when bitching about the Yankees' payroll.

Two airbags aren't safe enough. Six is better.

You find nothing particularly offensive about that video game. It's not like it's a documentary.

You don't see race everywhere you look. Can't we move on?

What's really wrong with the country is all this political correctness.

You get a tingle when you pay a bill. *That takes care of that!*

You need a house that's just a little bigger. Just a little bigger. Just a little—

Tap water works for you.

Having the same webcam girl for a month counts as a long-term relationship, of sorts.

You can name two Journey songs, not counting the one Tony Soprano played in the diner.

Growth can only be a good thing.

You secretly really enjoyed *Mamma Mia!* The '70s were actually kind of fun.

You think Halle Berry is hot. Okay, this makes you a guy.

You're vaguely uncomfortable using the word "motherfuckers."

You've never batted an eye at the fact that one of the priorities of the U.S. Constitution is the pursuit of happiness.

The cheque will clear. It always has.

You don't recall dancing during this decade—not once.

You see nothing particularly odd about not having kids. They're so expensive!

You need some visual proof before you're gonna believe there's a God.

You think Brett Favre is God. Okay. That'll do for visual proof.

You never learned to cook because it just never occurred to you.

You think it will all work out in the end—and then it does.

ACKNOWLEDGEMENTS

. . .

THIS BOOK STARTED LIFE in 1993 as a seven-minute monologue that I wrote in a class taught by the late Curt Dempster,
the founder of the Ensemble Studio Theatre in New York. Along
the way to becoming this book, *The White Guy* has had many mid-
wives. If this was an Oscar acceptance speech, I would say there
are too many to mention—but it's not an Oscar speech, it's a trade
paperback!

So thanks to all the directors, producers, development people,
managers and pals who helped at various stages as *The White Guy*
grew from monologue to man. That includes John Wulp, Terumi
Matthews, Wendy Fried, Eileen Myers, Marcia Jean Kurtz, Sue
Wolf, Jamie Richards, Shelby Jiggetts, George Wolf, Daria Overby,
Melissa Murray-Mutch, Kevin Mutch, Sarah Condon, Karyn Par-
sons, Quincy Jones, David Auerbach, Bob Read, Brian Daly, Kevin
Patterson, Todd Babiak and Mark Jenkins, among many others.

Many thanks to Scott Steedman, my editor, for enduring an
endless barrage of white guy jokes that left us both punchy by the
end. Thanks to Kevin Mutch for the wonderful cover and the white
guys who guard over each chapter.

Thanks again to my wife Melanee for being compulsively
expository and allowing me to peer into her inner thoughts. And
thanks to Carolyn, for being the coolest mother-in-law ever.

Thanks to *The Herald* for being a good place to work, with particular props for Monica Zurowski, Steve Jenkinson, Lorne Motley
and Tom Babin.

And thanks to Mom and Dad for being a good mom and dad.

One more: thanks to New York, whose deep dark secret is that
it's full of wonderful souls.

ABOUT THE AUTHOR

. . .

STEPHEN HUNT has had a number of plays produced Off Broadway, including *The White Guy*, produced in 1995 at the Public Theatre in New York and at the HBO Workspace in L.A., and developed for television by Warner Brothers and Quincy Jones in 2000. As a journalist, Hunt has covered arts and entertainment for the *Globe and Mail*, *New York Post*, the *Los Angeles Times*, the *New York Press*, *Saturday Night*, the CBC, National Public Radio and Britain's *FQ*, among many others. He's a graduate of the University of British Columbia's MFA program in creative writing and taught playwriting in their Optional Residency Program in 2007–08. Hunt has also studied at Playwrights Horizons in New York, the Ensemble Studio Theatre (where he's a member) and the Banff Centre for the Fine Arts, where he participated in the Cultural Journalism Program in 2004.

Currently, he is an entertainment reporter for *The Calgary Herald*; he has lived in Calgary, with his wife, Melanee, and five-year-old son, Gus, since 2006.